If
I Only
Knew...

Foreword by Roland S. Barth

Harvey B. Alvy
Pam Robbins

If I Only Knew...

Success Strategies for Navigating the Principalship

CORWIN PRESS, INC.
A Sage Publications Company
Thousand Oaks, California

For information:

Corwin Press, Inc.
A Sage Publications Company
2455 Teller Road
Thousand Oaks, California 91320
E-mail: order@corwinpress.com

SAGE Publications Ltd.
6 Bonhill Street
London EC2A 4PU
United Kingdom

SAGE Publications India Pvt. Ltd.
M-32 Market
Greater Kailash I
New Delhi 110 048 India

Printed in the United States of America

Library of Congress Cataloging-in-Publication Data

Alvy, Harvey B.
    If I only knew . . . : Success strategies for navigating the principalship / by Harvey B. Alvy and Pam Robbins.
        p. cm.
    Includes bibliographical references and index.
    ISBN 0-8039-6643-1 (cloth: acid-free paper)—
    ISBN 0-8039-6644-X (pbk.: acid-free paper)
        1. School principals—United States. 2. School management and organization—United States. I. Robbins, Pamela. II. Title.
    LB2831.92.A58 1998
    371.2′012—dc21   97-45423

This book is printed on acid-free paper.

03 10 9 8 7 6 5

Production Editor: Sherrise Purdum
Production Assistant: Denise Santoyo
Designer/Typesetter: Rebecca Evans
Editorial Assistant: Kristen L. Gibson

To Bonnie, Ray, and Rebecca

CORWIN
PRESS

The Corwin Press logo—a raven striding across an open book— represents the happy union of courage and learning. We are a professional-level publisher of books and journals for K–12 educators, and we are committed to creating and providing resources that embody these qualities. Corwin's motto is "Success for All Learners."

Contents

Foreword

During the years I directed the Principals' Center at Harvard University, it was one of my most important goals to identify principals from the Boston area who were very good at something and then invite them to discuss and disclose their strengths to other principals who wanted to *become* good at that. A logical and simple, even potent, form of professional development I thought.

Well not so simple, actually. In the first place schoolpeople, placed in the cruel situation where they must fight for scarce resources and recognition, can be a very competitive lot. If I share what I know about involving parents with you, more parents may send their children to your school—and mine may close. Better not share.

Secondly, there is a taboo in the school culture against one practitioner sharing what he or she knows with another—as many teachers who have stood up in a faculty meeting to convey a good idea, and been met with put-downs like, "Who does she think *she* is?" "What's she looking for, a promotion? Big deal. We did that 20 years ago."

For these reasons, many school practitioners keep their abundant craft knowledge to themselves, like high cards held closely to the vest. What a tragic loss—for everyone.

Additionally, I discovered that when I invited an incontrovertibly accomplished principal to address a group of colleagues about, say, the Glasser discipline methods, many who were so good at *doing* it in their schools were not very good at conveying it to others. The skills involved in practicing it, are very different than the skills of reflecting on practice, clarifying practice, and articulating and imparting good practice to others.

In this tidy little volume you are about to read, you will find two educators who have labored long and hard within the schools and with schoolpeople from other schools. They have developed an impressive knowledge base of their craft wisdom. And here, they have chosen to disclose to us what they have learned along the way, in particular, about the important work of the school principal.

Harvey Alvy and Pam Robbins, both veterans of the art form known as "school leadership," have much to give to new principals. They know both how to do it and how to convey to others what has been successful in their experience.

By "new principals," the authors mean both the novice, beginning principals, and the experienced school leaders who find themselves in new settings. This is an interesting mix of audiences . . . one that should interact more often. For there is no more crucial role for all principals than to engage in, celebrate and model the most central enterprise of the schoolhouse—human learning.

I find in *If I Only Knew* . . . , an encyclopedic compilation of insights on the major issues confronting school principals—from acknowledging veteran teachers to dealing with leaky toilets. Suggestions put forth are concrete, sensible, and approachable, offered with rich texture and description. Like any encyclopedia, this work is best read, not cover to cover, but selectively. Want to know about grievances? Look up and read "Grievances and the School Principal."

You will find here, not only the voices of two reflective practitioners but the voices of scores of introspective principals, who in their own words, frame and ponder their problematic issues. What they have to say resonates all too well with my own lumpy attempts at being a "new principal" in three different school settings.

How does one prepare for one of the most important and difficult positions in our society? By taking courses. By observing mentors. By learning on the job. By talking with other principals. And by reading about it.

I remember a high school principal in Michigan once saying, "It is not the height of the mountains that does me in but the pebbles in my shoes."

There are countless books written to prepare principals, on principals, for principals, and about principals. This one is a wonderful antidote for those pebbles in the principals' shoes.

Roland S. Barth
December 1997

Preface

Purpose of the Book

Originally, we intended this book for rookie and aspiring principals. But as we began writing, we were struck by the reality that each time any principal—rookie or veteran—is assigned to a new principalship or building (i.e., an entire school being moved to a new campus), he or she is, in fact, new again. Moreover, all principals occasionally need to take a fresh look at their performance to revitalize their commitment, reexamine their missions, and review the bigger picture of their schools, colleagues, students, and communities.

All of us have reflected, "If I only knew that before I started, I could have accomplished so much more." A key purpose of this book is to give an "insider's view" of the many dimensions that affect the lives of principals. These dimensions provide a perspective of principals' early experiences including the problems, challenges, frustrations, and socialization process that newcomers experience as well as those dilemmas and issues that both new and veteran principals encounter. With this in mind, the chapters that follow offer guidelines, checklists, sage advice from other principals, considerations, and reflections to make any principal's day on the job run more smoothly. To the extent that one can ponder these ideas, strategies, and techniques proactively, in some cases it might save time and foster being ready ahead of time for things that "come up." "Glitches" will be better anticipated.

In addition to the knowledge base provided in the book, the content also serves as a guide to what one might anticipate as well as a source of consolation; that is, the principal often in a sea of difficult circumstances wonders, "Is something wrong with my leadership style? Does anyone else encounter these problems?" As others encounter the mantle of leadership, their challenges will be portrayed, as will the strategies that both newcomers and veterans have found to work in the face of these problems. Finally, pointers will be offered that will ease and enable the path to positive, enduring, and successful leadership.

What We Bring as Authors to This Book

As with our previous book, *The Principal's Companion,* we think our combination of experiences gives us a unique perspective and expertise to talk about both the newcomer to the principalship and the veteran who finds himself or herself in a new school setting.

In 1980, Harvey Alvy began to seriously study the problems of new principals for a very practical reason: He was preparing for the principalship. Surprisingly, at the time, there was very little written about the topic (Gorton, 1980). He studied the topic carefully since then but waited to write a comprehensive and reflective view of the topic until he experienced the principalship for several years. The reason was simple: He wanted to find out, firsthand, what the problems of principals were and how he would, hopefully, mature in the position. To write a comprehensive book about the principalship without experiencing the position seemed to be like writing about the excitement of a roller coaster ride without ever riding one. The resulting view is unique. Although Alvy was well grounded on content knowledge about the principalship before entering the field, on the job he discovered what parts of the content knowledge were helpful. He viewed the experience as a reflective journey that he hoped to share with others some day. He has since served as both an elementary and a secondary school principal. Presently, he is the high school principal of the Singapore American School. Although serving in the principalship for more than a decade, he is new, again, in taking on the principalship in Singapore. He can be reached at the Singapore American School, 40 Woodlands Street #41, Singapore 738547; by phone (011-65) 360-6521; and by e-mail (halvy@sas.edu.sg).

Pam Robbins has had the unique experience of observing and working with principals for the past 26 years. As a child, she experienced the trials and tribulations of the principalship through the eyes of her father, an elementary school principal. She has worked with principals throughout the world and has designed, developed, and delivered training for several principals' academies. In addition, for several years, she facilitated an ongoing support group for principals in which newcomers and seasoned professionals came together to problem solve, share successes, and support one another. During the early 1980s, she worked with the Peer Assisted Leadership Program operating out of the Far West Laboratory for Educational Research in San Francisco. This project was designed as a shadowing experience for principals to develop understanding skills and a base of collegial support. Robbins also served as director of training for the North Bay California School Leadership Academy. She now operates as an independent consultant, working with schools, districts, and professional organizations throughout the United States, Canada, Great Britain, Europe, and the Far East. She can be reached at 1251 Windsor Lane, Mt. Crawford, VA 22841; by phone (540) 828-0107; and by e-mail (probbins@shentel.net).

This book combines the experiences of Alvy and Robbins, the ideas of others who have researched the principalship, and the views of a legion of principals whose ideas, and often exact words, give us a portrait of the problems, challenges, and opportunities encountered by school leaders. Collectively, this sage advice is designed to facilitate the transition to successful educational leadership.

Donmoyer, Imber, and Scheurich (1995), in *The Knowledge Base in Educational Administration*, reflect that "today there is a growing realization that no knowledge is objective and that all knowing reflects the values, interests, and biases of the knower" (pp. 5-6). There is no one model of successful leadership. Rather, the skillful educational leader enacts those practices that are consistent with his or her belief systems, compatible with his or her style, and effective in the context in which they are played out. This book represents a collection of behaviors, stories, and practices from which one can select to reflect his or her own unique "values, interests, and biases" in pursuing the vision of the principal.

Critical Themes

In addition to the main parts of the book, which will be discussed shortly, several themes or threads will be stressed throughout the text. These themes include (a) school administration as a human relations enterprise, (b) increasing our awareness of the principal's socialization process, (c) the leader as a lifelong learner, (d) viewing the

school as an ecosystem, (e) purposeful visibility, (f) organizational
ethical alignment, (g) celebrating student and faculty achievements,
and (h) the principal as a leader of instructional leaders. Although
each of these themes could stand on its own as a chapter topic, each
theme is instead woven into the fabric of the text to help form a vision
of school leadership. A few comments about each theme follow.

Human relations and school administration. More than 40 years ago,
in a seminal work on school administration, Coladarci and Getzels
(1955) stressed that administration is the study of human relations.
The principalship is a "people" profession, and no degree of expertise in instructional, curricular, budgetary, or time management skills
is going to make principals successful if they lack the ability to communicate honestly with students, faculty, classified staff, parents, and
the broader community. Principals work on problems, challenges,
and opportunities each day. These activities demand communication
among individuals. Through effective human relations skills, the
communication process can lead to successful resolution of most
challenges experienced in our schools.

Socialization as a school principal. Principalship socialization is a
growth process. The principal begins as a rookie and increases his or
her skills on the job, becoming an experienced principal as the principalship tenure increases by days, weeks, and years. Increasing
one's awareness of the socialization *process* and considering ways in
which to help newcomers through the process is a vital goal of this
book. One does not become a seasoned veteran principal overnight,
although beginning principals do have the same responsibilities as
do the veterans from the first moment on the job. There are different
socialization models that can be used to describe the newcomer process (Daresh, 1993; Hart, 1993; Louis, 1980; Schein, 1974). In Chapter 1, an effective socialization model will be described to help principals understand their personal evolutionary experience.

Leader as lifelong learner. Individuals who become principals intend to be the best principals they can be. This requires continuous
growth, absorbing new ideas, and consistently asking questions to
gain greater understanding. The habit of continuous learning, the
notion of the leader as learner, is an essential theme of this book.

School principals should set an example of growth, not only for personal development but also to serve as an effective role model for students, teachers, and parents.

The school as an ecosystem. An ecosystem operates by creating a balance among the different parts of the system. This conception infers that problems in one part of the system can affect other parts of the system. The concept of ecosystem certainly applies to schools. In schools, building a climate of growth means creating trust, risk taking, dialogue, and collaboration among the various parts of the ecosystem. School principals, sensitive to this concept, should recognize that although they might have first-rate skills in directing a curriculum review cycle, these skills can be meaningless if teachers fear attempting new teaching strategies necessary to implement a new curriculum approach.

Purposeful visibility. The school leader should be visible in classrooms, in hallways, on the playground, in the cafeteria, at faculty workshops . . . and the list goes on. The symbolic presence of the leader at school events, both routine and special, sends a message that the heart of the school is where the students are, not the principal's office. Techniques such as management and leadership by wandering around should be used systematically by the principal so that the students, teachers, and community know that the principal cares, is "out there," and is where the action is.

Organizational ethical alignment. It seems that all organizations today are facing the challenge of ethical leadership. The principalship is no different, as new and veteran principals strive to provide ethical leadership. A key theme discussed throughout this book is how principals, both new and veteran, must strive to ensure that their organizations are "ethically aligned." Ethical alignment is defined as creating an organizational culture in which ethical decisions about people—concerned with teaching, learning, and democratic actions—can be observed throughout the organization. These ethical decisions can be observed in classrooms, in the principal's office, in daily relations between and among adults and students, during staff activities, in interactions with parents and the larger community, and in how the school facility is used.

Celebrating student and faculty achievements. It is motivating to know that progess is being made. The school principal, as the official leader of the school, should let students and teachers know when they have achieved success and should build a capacity within individuals to recognize and celebrate their own accomplishments as the success relates to the school mission. The recognition of success and specific accomplishments is a way of celebrating what is important for the school and helps to bind the culture around significant accomplishments. Moreover, the word *celebration* is critical as a metaphor of mutual pleasure in the accomplishments of others. The celebrations can be at faculty meetings, at assemblies, at parent meetings, at open houses, in class, in the halls, or in the community. What is important is that success is recognized and revered.

The principal as instructional leader. During the 1990s, several influential organizations have devoted considerable effort into the development of documents that include guidelines, domains, or indicators for school principals and educational administration programs to help identify key leadership characteristics. These documents have been developed by the National Policy Board for Educational Administration, the National Council for Accreditation of Teacher Education (NCATE), and the Interstate School Leaders Licensure Consortium (ISLLC). A primary theme in all these documents is the principal's role as a school visionary who combines management and instructional leadership skills to positively affect student learning and teacher professional growth. Neil Shipman, project director of the ISLLC effort, emphasizes the strong congruence between the NCATE and ISLLC works and that "truly effective leaders are involved in instructional issues" (Willis, 1996, p. 4).

The instructional leadership role of the principal certainly has been emphasized in the educational administration literature. More important, however, it has now become a significant part of the everyday behavior of school principals. Brubaker (1995) has collected biographies of principals for more than 20 years and stresses that the biographies indicate that principals today view themselves as instructional leaders, not just managers. Thus, a major theme of this book is to consistently emphasize the principal's role as an instructional leader while recognizing that the managerial responsibilities cannot be overlooked.

How the Book Is Organized

Part I, "The Challenges and Problems Facing Rookie and Veteran Principals New to Their Schools," begins with an examination of sociological factors that affect all principals and background issues, such as one's personal history and professional teaching experience, that certainly influence one's performance. This section stresses that principals do not have the luxury of learning slowly on the job and addresses the compelling notion that one's behavior during the first year might be a strong indicator of future success. Part I then describes several challenging problem areas that concern principals making transitions. These include loneliness, the time juggernaut, expectations of the instructional leader, the complexity of relationships, and management concerns such as budgetary, legal, union, and facility issues. Two premises guiding Part I are that (a) principals value knowing what they should expect on the job and (b) principals must first identify problems before solving problems.

Part II, "Finding Solutions to the Challenges and Problems: Strategies, Advice, and Insights for Success," is loaded with ideas to help principals move through the transitional period in their new school settings. This section provides ideas to help overcome many of the problems discussed previously. These ideas include becoming a lifelong learner, internalizing the principalship socialization process, exercising skills in human relations and communication, honoring the experienced staff, balancing leadership and management, school law, collective bargaining and grievance procedures, proactive behavioral strategies, and developing a vision for teaching and learning. The book concludes with a chapter titled "The Obvious Is Not Always Obvious: What School Principals Often Forget." This chapter describes aspects of the principalship that should be obvious but sometimes are overlooked. For example, principals can become so engrossed in trying to make a difference in the lives of students that they can forget that adults in schools also have needs. In addition, this final chapter discusses the moral responsibilities of the school principal in an ethically aligned organization.

If you visualize a glass half-empty when reading Part I of the book, then visualize the same glass as overflowing with ideas in Part II to help you succeed as a principal. We hope that this book will support principals in doing what they do best—touching the lives of those in and around their schools.

Acknowledgments

If I Only Knew . . . could not have been written without the candid comments of dedicated principals throughout the United States and abroad. Many of these individuals, in their first or second year of the principalship, opened up to us, to reveal their personal reflections and anxieties about their decisions and roles. These honest comments will help others who will serve in the principalship.

Additionally, we would like to thank Gracia Alkema, the President of Corwin Press, for her confidence in us and support throughout the project. Our production editor, Sherrise Purdum, should also be acknowledged for adding the final touches to ensure that the book would be completed.

Introduction:
A Veteran Principal Finds
Himself or Herself New, Again

Why is it that after serving more than a decade in the principalship, one still feels like a newcomer when accepting and beginning a principalship in a different school? The old questions surface. Will I succeed? Will I have to prove myself again? Have any faculty members, students, or parents in the new school heard about my work in my previous position?

Veteran principals moving to new schools quietly reflect. Will I be making the mistakes, again, that all new principals make? Can I sustain the patience, observation skills, sensitivities, and talent for remembering names and interests necessary to go through the "getting-to-know-you" period? Principals rely on a school's veteran and experienced teachers, secretaries, and maintenance personnel during their first principalships. Once more, reliance on these critical individuals is necessary. Other newcomer challenges will have to be addressed. Some of the challenges might seem minor, but they are not minor to newcomers. For example, what time is it appropriate to arrive at the office? What is the best route to work? Will I have to learn new software programs for scheduling, discipline, attendance, student records, and so on? (Undoubtedly, yes.)

As the old anxieties surface, one can reduce stress and tension by reminding oneself of important newcomer responsibilities that should be carried out before the new school year begins. A major goal of this book is to present the reader with ideas and strategies to begin the school year smoothly. However, to give the newcomer an initial feel for some of these leadership and management responsibilities, consider the following beginning-of-the-year "to do" list for rookie and seasoned principals taking on new principalships. The list includes leadership, logistical/management, student services, personnel, curricular/instructional, and communication responsibilities.

Leadership

- Write, review, or rewrite one's personal mission/vision about the principalship. What counts? What should I stand for? How can I quickly communicate the vision to the school community through my everyday actions?
- If possible, spend time with the principal you are replacing. Shadow this person. What do the actions you observe communicate? What do the words convey? What has been the principal's "agenda"? What are the logistical "glitches" that need to be resolved for the new school year?
- Review the immediate goals that the school has set for the new school year. Are there long-range goals? Are there key personnel involved? Try to spend time with these individuals before the year begins.
- Review the economic and social characteristics of the local school and the greater community. What type of jobs do parents hold? What percentage of the students receive free or reduced lunch? What are the higher education, vocational/technical, and military service expectations of the community?
- Introduce yourself with a "welcome back" letter to teachers.

Logistical/Management

- Read the district/school philosophy statements, policies, and procedures and the specific school rules and regulations. Have a copy of the appropriate state codes.
- Examine the school budget. If possible, review the budget with the appropriate district officer. Does the budget align with the educational needs of the school? How is the district/school budget cycle implemented? What type of fiscal author-

ity will the principal have during the year? What are the building purchasing and accounting procedures?

- With the secretary, review the "tickler" file of each month's key events with appropriate memos (if the school has a tickler file) and the activity calendar for the school year to get a feel for the school's yearly rhythm. If a tickler file is not in place, then begin one as soon as possible with the help of the secretary.

- How are student and faculty books and instructional supplies distributed? Are the instructional orders on target for the new school year? Traditionally, who has been in charge of this process in the district—the school? Make sure that each teacher receives a minimum of instructional materials, grade books, and office supplies to begin the year.

- Make sure that furniture and fixtures in each classroom are satisfactory. Are there enough student desks? Student chairs? Faculty desks? Faculty chairs? Are the lights working properly? Window blinds? Electrical outlets? White boards?

- Review frequently used school and district forms with the secretary and other key personnel.

- Familiarize yourself with school board procedures and board expectations of the principals.

- Review health, safety, and security standards in the school with appropriate personnel.

- Develop an easy access location for critical phone numbers—fire, ambulance, police, rescue squad, and the like.

- Meet with the appropriate secretaries and develop systems to prioritize activities to open school smoothly. Ask questions. How was it done last year? What worked? What did not work? Discuss the importance of avoiding isolation in the principal's office and the importance of communicating that the principal's responsibility is to serve students, teachers, and parents. Review your time management strategies with the secretary. Ask the secretary to share his or hers.

- Walk through the school with the custodian. Stress with the custodian the importance of taking pride in a clean and safe school. Walk through the school alone (have master keys made).

- Spend time with key transportation and food service personnel. Learn schedules and concerns.

- Prepare signs to help on the first day of school.

Student Services

- Review grade and testing data for the school. How does the school "compare" with other schools in the district? What seems to be the strengths? Areas that need improvement? Special testing programs? When are important standardized tests scheduled for the year?
- Familiarize yourself with the student handbook and specific school rules and regulations (e.g., discipline, dress code, lateness, athletic code).
- What are the student disciplinary procedures? Is a workable system in place for severe violations, suspensions, and expulsions?
- What activities or programs have been institutionalized in the school to affirm student success?
- How does the student government operate? Who are the faculty advisers? How has the principal previously interacted with the student government? How are student activity funds handled?
- Is there an orientation program for new students? Who has been involved in the past? Are they on board for this year?
- If possible, meet with the specialist staff before school. Meet especially with guidance personnel to review student schedules, special programs, policies for special education, community services, and the like.

Personnel

- Does the school have assistant/vice principals, department chairs, lead teachers, or program directors? If it does, then review responsibilities and make sure that individuals with leadership responsibilities know that you will respect and work closely with them from Day 1. If possible, begin building the relationship with the assistant/vice principals during the summer.
- Review the district collective bargaining agreement and familiarize yourself with district grievance procedures.
- Does the school have an orientation program and buddy system for new teachers? Who can help implement the plan this

year? Have the new teachers been given the appropriate curriculum documents? Personnel handbooks?

- Are there last-minute faculty openings that need to be filled? What is the district interview procedure for these openings?
- What is the school procedure for notifying, assigning, and orienting substitute teachers?

Curricular/Instructional

- Review the district/school curriculum documents. Is the scope and sequence aligned? Are the documents current? Do teachers have copies of appropriate documents?
- Examine the master schedule for students and faculty. For a middle or high school, review typical student schedules. Review faculty grade level, subject, and room assignments. Have conflicts been resolved? What are the projected enrollment figures? If enrollment increases or decreases considerably, what will be the implications for staffing, facility use, and the master schedule?
- Does the district/school have a technology plan? Meet with key district/school technology personnel to learn about current resources and future objectives.
- Review the staff development and evaluation program. What is the process and time line for the faculty evaluation system? How are teacher and school professional growth plans developed? What is the evaluation program for new teachers?
- Prepare for the faculty meetings. Make sure that refreshments are available.

Communication

- How is daily communication with staff conducted? With students?
- Meet with a few veteran faculty members during the summer to find out about the school's history. Try to determine the sacred cows and traps to avoid.
- Meet with officers of the parent organization. Discuss how communication with parents and the community was carried

out in previous years. What are the procedures for orienting
new parents to the school?

- Examine newsletters and memos that have been sent out to
parents. Has the communication been monthly? Weekly?
- Begin to develop relationships with community service and
business organizations through personal contact, phone calls,
and letters.

All the items on this "to do" list will be elaborated on in the following chapters. To successfully open their schools, all principals—
both rookies and veterans—will need to do activities similar to those
just listed.

List additional things to do in the space below:

PART ONE

The Challenges and Problems Facing Rookie and Veteran Principals New to Their Schools

The chapters in this part emphasize challenges and problems that are unique to principals attempting to execute responsibilities in new settings or situations. These problems often are accentuated because of inexperience. To illustrate, all principals know that one can feel very lonely in the position. Yet, the loneliness might come as a surprise, especially for the newcomer who was hired "in district" or for the individual who was hired in the same school in which he or she had taught. Skelly (1996), a veteran principal, reflected, "My years of work as an assistant principal and as a teacher did not prepare me for the distance from others that I experienced" (p. 91).

Principals frequently comment that the problems and challenges of today are much more complicated than in the past. There is some evidence that principal responsibilities have increased over the years (Wulff, 1996). Many principalship experts state that the job has become more complex—especially since the 1980s—because of disruptive social dynamics, a decline in financial resources, and changes in family structures. Today there are greater drug and alcohol use, an increase in violent crimes, more students in nontraditional homes, fiscal belt tightening, the complexity of site-based decisions, less respect for school leaders, greater diversity of students and languages, and the challenge of charter schools.

Fortunately, today's principals have an enhanced knowledge base from which to operate. The expanding research

regarding brain functioning provides rich insights for instruction and resources to support the teaching and learning process. Technology has emerged as a valuable tool to facilitate
curriculum and instruction as well as to improve communication. In these chapters, as we examine the challenges facing principals in transition, we should consider how new and
seasoned veterans can look to each other for support, resources, and problem-solving strategies to effectively serve
students, teachers, and the community.

CHAPTER 1

Factors That Affect Rookie and Veteran Principals Changing School Settings

> What we know always has something to do with who we are, where we have been, who has socialized us, and what we believe.
>
> *Donmoyer, Imber, and Scheurich (1995, p. 3)*

When one enters the principalship, several factors and phenomena that will affect performance already are in place. To gain a greater understanding of what awaits the principal and what the principal brings to the job, let us spend a few minutes examining these factors. This examination should help principals understand some of their initial encounters. Anxiety-producing experiences can be viewed as universal newcomer experiences. This examination also should help newcomers reflect on what they bring to the principalship, acknowledge the value of the newcomers' lens, and feel empowered to address several administrative challenges.

The Common Experiences of Newcomers

Newcomers to any situation experience conditions that affect how they will behave. For example, newcomers often feel vulnerable because they are unsure of how the new system or operation works as they are "learning the ropes." Newcomers often exhibit a greater dependence on others at this time. School secretaries frequently play a major role in orienting and supporting principals during the first few years of service. This beginning period also is a time when principals are careful observers; the "antennas" are up much more than usual as new elements stimulating the senses are taken in (Duke, Isaacson, Sagor, & Schmuck, 1984).

For example, even mundane acts such as turning a key in a door, operating a copier machine, figuring out the phone system, and using e-mail initially can be "challenging" experiences. In time, these acts become easy and routine. Each new job has hundreds of these mundane tasks that take time and must be learned for one's comfort level to settle. Later, a principal can gain "a little respect" for fixing that copier for the teacher who is on the run and needs to make 30 copies before the next class (not great planning, but reality). On a more sophisticated level, a principal must learn the district budget timeline and the type of curriculum review cycle used in the district. Then there are the more subtle elements that the newcomer needs to learn such as the verbal and nonverbal cues and behaviors of colleagues; for example, when is a good time to ask Mr. Smith to become involved with a major project?

The Socialization Process

The transition period from the time one is appointed as a principal until one becomes accepted in the organization has been labeled by sociologists as the "organizational socialization period." Although many organizational socialization developmental models have been created (Hart, 1993), the following three-stage model makes the most sense. These three stages of development for the newcomer period are (a) the anticipatory socialization stage, (b) the encounter stage, and (c) the insider stage (Louis, 1980; Schein, 1974). The anticipatory socialization stage begins when you have been selected as a principal and have made the decision to leave your present position (and likely your present school) and take the new job. This stage is characterized by breaking off your loyalties to your present organization (e.g., "I never really liked working here anyway") and developing new loyalties (e.g., "I always wanted to work in this capacity"). This experience—psychologically cutting off the ties—is referred to as "leave taking" (Louis, 1980).

When you accept a new job, "healthy leave taking" probably is occurring if you are looking forward to the new position but have fond memories of your present position. When someone is unsuccessful in a new job, a possible cause might be an inability to separate from the past, possibly romanticizing about how wonderful that previous position was (e.g., "I should have remained a teacher. The problems of a principal are never ending. When am I going to have a day off?").

The encounter stage begins when you actually start the new job and cope with the routines, surprises, and relationships of the position. This book is largely about succeeding during the encounter stage. How quickly you enter the insider stage can be an indicator of how well you have traveled through the encounter stage.

The insider stage begins when you develop strong trusting relationships in the schoolhouse, are accepted in the organization, and find out how things work in the informal organization (e.g., "So, Ms. Smith is the teacher I need to check with before speaking with the superintendent about the new curriculum idea"). According to Duke et al. (1984, p. 12), the induction period for both new and veteran principals is relatively short. Within a few months, new principals are accepted by the community and students; by the end of the first year, they are accepted by most "reference" groups. Another indicator of insider stage "success" is when a principal has developed a network of colleagues—individuals whom one looks forward to seeing at district principalship meetings, social functions, and state or national association meetings.

Assessing One's Personal and Professional Background: What Do I Bring to the Job?

The context of one's personal and professional experience is different for each individual and, to a great extent, will dictate one's style of leadership. When one accepts a principalship, good and bad "baggage" is carried to the position. The context of past experience will, to some extent, dictate how successfully one will respond to the challenges of the principalship. Problem-solving capacities differ. When

seemingly unsolvable problems occur, one often needs the synergis-
tic ideas of the group to achieve success. Yet, an individual's desire
or ability to bring together colleagues to resolve a problem might
depend on one's background. Does the principal work well with
groups? Does the principal prefer, based on personal experience, to
confide in only one person? Is the principal willing to say "I need
help"? Most likely, a new principal—in fact any principal—will
achieve much greater success if collaboration is used to solve challenges. Unfortunately, not everyone who comes to the principalship
brings that experience or comfort level with him or her.

To carefully assess and reflect on how background influences on-
the-job performance, let us examine four areas: personal characteristics, past experiences as a teacher, preservice and university training, and administrative experience. After reviewing these background
factors, consider the implications for the principalship position you
recently have accepted, are presently serving in, or hope to obtain.
For example, is your background a "good match" with the school
you presently are serving or will be serving? If not, then what do you
need to do to create a stronger match? Will you be flexible and able
to serve in a variety of situations? Do you think an open-door policy
will fit your style? Will a high-profile, visible type of principalship
style suit you? Do you think your style will tend to be autocratic,
democratic, laissez-faire, or empowering?

Personal Characteristics

Each individual brings a different background and career path
to the principalship. Background factors include cultural heritage,
family experiences, gender, tolerance for change, and personality
style. This has implications for the type of setting in which one will
experience success—urban, rural, or suburban. Does one have the
skills to serve in a multicultural setting? How will one's personality
suit a school that has been led for the past 10 years by "Ms. Totally
Organized"? Does humor come easy? (A light moment sure can help
to reduce tension during a parent conference or faculty meeting.)

Miklos (1988, p. 61) reports that principals from ethnic minority
groups tend to be placed in schools with high proportions of students
from similar ethnic or cultural backgrounds. This raises the issue of
how one might self-select or be selected by others for a match that
diminishes the need to "educate" oneself about the cultural heritage

of a community. However, little might be gained by the "cultural heritage match" if that match diminishes the diversity and creativity that can prosper when different worldviews are brought together.

Miklos (1988) also suggests that geographic mobility tends to enhance one's career (p. 63). Certainly, some individuals have the personal capacity or desire to relocate. Others prefer the familiar nest of home. When one prefers a particular locale, opportunities might be limited. As a result, some potentially "great principals" never will have the opportunity to serve because of these preferences for geographic locations.

One's own formal schooling experiences also play a key role in the principalship. Think about your schooling. What type of pupil were you? What was your favorite subject? Did you make frequent visits to the principal's office? For what reasons? What were the images of the principalship that you encountered? What were the messages your school sent to you? If you were female, were you encouraged to take, or dissuaded from taking, math or science? Was writing or public speaking valued? How were sports viewed? Was reflection encouraged? Collectively, these experiences—positive or negative—usually influence one's behavior and ultimately one's success in the principalship.

Past Experience as a Teacher

When one becomes a school principal, there always is the feeling that to gain credibility with the staff and to feel confident about giving advice on teaching, one should be able to sincerely state, "I was a good teacher." If the word is out among the faculty (especially if you are hired from within a district) that you were a good teacher, then you likely will begin your administrative career with some credibility among the staff. How will your teaching experience be reflected in the principalship? Factors that might carry over from teaching include the climate and culture of the school. For example, was the climate healthy? Was it intimidating? Did you work in a school in which teachers were comfortable sharing successes and failures? Or, was your school one in which isolation was the norm?

How successful were you as a teacher? What type of relationship did you have with your supervisor when you were a teacher? To what models of supervision were you exposed? As a result of your experience, what do you think of the supervision process? If your supervision experience was unpleasant, are you going to recoil from the supervision process? Were you territorial about your own classroom? Did you resent it when someone—especially the principal—"invaded" your territory? What type of principal models have you observed? Hopefully, you have worked with some excellent principals who will serve as exemplary role models. What type of relationships did you have with other teachers, the classified staff, and parents? Most important, what type of relationship did you have with students?

Another essential consideration is your area of teaching expertise. You might be a content area specialist such as an elementary reading specialist, a middle school physical education specialist, a high school guidance counselor, a science specialist, or an advanced placement calculus specialist. You might be an elementary generalist or a middle or high school teacher who has taught several different subjects during your career. With the emphasis on technology, you might have an edge as a candidate for the principalship if you have a strong technology background. However, will you be an open-minded advocate of new musical instruments, instead of technological resources, if there is a greater student need for musical resources? As this example points out, one of the challenges of the principalship is to take a broad view of a school's needs beyond one's area of expertise.

University Preparation

What about preparatory training for the principalship? Could it realistically prepare you? Some observers of the principalship maintain that one learns the job only while serving in the principalship. Garberina (1980) suggests that "despite university efforts to certify thousands of aspiring principals, their programs alone will never be sufficient, if only because no one knows what the principal will face until the situation or problem presents itself" (p. 6).

A university professor, training school principals, constantly has to provide knowledge and activities that can help prospective administrators develop a conception of the principalship. There constantly is an inner struggle between how much theory should be taught and how many practical activities should be emphasized. For example, an administrative class can be devoted solely to organizational behavior theories, leadership theories, and motivational theories. On the other hand, the course can emphasize practical activities such as case studies, simulations, role-playing, and in-basket exercises. Most professors use a combination of both theory and practice, but there is no guarantee for the prospective administrator that the course experience will be helpful.

Some literature indicates that principalship training is just the opposite of reality (Bridges, 1976; Sarason, 1982). In the university, you spend extended periods of time reflecting about a problem and solution; in the principalship, problem resolution was expected yesterday. In a university class, you might read a case study on searching a school locker for drugs and debate with classmates whether the search should be conducted. As a school principal, you might hear about possible drugs in a locker 10 minutes before afternoon dismissal; you need to act quickly. In a supervision class, you might go through the steps in recommending that a teacher be dismissed and receive an "A" on your final exam for correctly reviewing the steps with time lines. However, the course requirements do not include the emotional drain, soul searching, time, and one other critical detail— the face of that teacher.

Principals' voices:

There wasn't any real guts-and-blood sorts of things encountered [in university classes]. . . . Nothing is real hands-on experience, as far as I've seen. It's philosophical.

The university covers philosophy beautifully. But also I'm a reader, so there wasn't a tremendous amount of new knowledge there. But the practicality . . . How do you, in fact, handle angry teachers or the lunchroom? never entered my mind. [Nor did] the chaos that goes on in the lunchroom. What do you do if a school hasn't set up a discipline policy and you come on board?

Another critical element is the type of administrative internship you experienced as part of your graduate preparation. Each state has different requirements, but in most cases you need to serve some type of internship or practicum to receive your certification. The quality and length of the internship experience can affect your success. A key part would be the type of mentor principal with whom you worked. Did the mentor, usually a practicing principal, take an active role in your development or simply give you responsibilities that he or she preferred not to do? At Eastern Washington University, students serving administrative internships in local schools felt like they were in a "gray area" given administrative responsibilities but not the official authority to implement their decisions (Alvy, 1997). Although the interns were generally satisfied with the broad range of experiences, some were saddled with a great deal of disciplinary responsibilities. Several interns, interestingly, enjoyed the disciplinary part because it gave them an opportunity to get to know certain students. These interns were quite pleased when a student's behavior improved significantly. Also, interns stressed the importance of being an active listener and a real "people person" in the principalship. Several interns expressed concern about the budgetary process and worried about their success as future fiscal managers.

One principal suggested:

Finding successful principals that are good in their field, bringing them on board [in the university], [and] letting them set you up. How do you start the new year out—you know, as a new person to a new district? What are the practical issues?

Interns and mentor principals believe that a major element in the success of one's internship is the quality of the mentor. Good role models help interns develop and implement productive ideas and strategies for their own principalships. Exceptional mentors provide interns with strategies and ideas to begin a school year, run faculty meetings, create master schedules, develop school handbooks, organize master calendars, develop disciplinary strategies, and work with veteran staff members, disgruntled parents, and new teachers. One mentor noted that the experience of working with an intern was rejuvenating and gave him someone to talk with. Many principals must realize this; Shelton (1991) reports that more than 90% of principals in a National Association of Elementary School Principals survey indicated a desire to serve as mentors.

Hart (1993) cautions us to avoid going overboard concerning the positive role that mentors and role models can play, especially when systemic change is necessary. Mentors are, of course, veteran principals and can represent the establishment and traditional thinking. Building on the work of Van Maanen and Schein, Hart suggested, "Mentors also constrain innovation. . . . Just as mentors can suppress innovation, role models can limit thinking and constrain options" (pp. 23, 26).

Graduate school training programs vary widely in the knowledge and skills they provide, the internships they coordinate, and the support they provide. Ultimately, the only true test of whether a graduate program is effective is how one performs on the job. Success is related to the preparatory schooling, experiences encountered, and one's interest, motivation, "stick-to-itiveness," and skill.

Previous Administrative Experiences

In most cases, new principals held administrative or "quasi-administrative" posts before their first principalships. The administrative ladder of positions might have included assistant principal, department chair, lead teacher, curriculum coordinator, guidance director, athletic director, school or district coordinator, migrant or English as a Second Language post, or a variety of other leadership roles. In any of these positions, one might work closely with a principal. Again, the quality of the mentor or role model can affect the intern's leadership potential. For example, what were the strengths and weaknesses of the principal with whom you worked? Did this person serve as an example by which to pattern your own principalship behaviors? In your preprincipalship administrative position, did you have good relationships with staff, students, and parents? Did you have a chance to engage in professional growth activities to improve your staff evaluation, budgetary, and curriculum development skills?

The jury is still out regarding whether particular administrative positions actually prepare one for the principalship. Blumberg and Greenfield (1980) reflect that the position of assistant principal responsible for discipline might actually be a dysfunctional role for the principalship because of the emphasis on the disciplinary side of the job. Hartzell, Williams, and Nelson (1995), studying first-year assistant principals, add an interesting twist to this point by stressing that 90% of high school assistant principals deal with discipline, whereas universities do not adequately train leaders for disciplinary responsibilities. University training programs often stress instructional supervision and leadership. Discipline typically is not perceived as part of these more visionary areas. Although behavior management is an essential element in the total picture of school success, many universities are finding that providing leaders with training in social and emotional learning both affects behavior and provides essential life skills.

The Administrative Ladder

Reflect, for a moment, on the organization and individuals who influenced your progress up the administrative ladder. Did the district promote you, or did you fight the tide and promote yourself without being "anointed"? Many female administrators have fought the "good ol' boys' network" to gain opportunities as principals. Lyman et al. (1993) stated, "Women had to do more and work harder than men in comparable positions to establish their credibility and professional competence" (p. 35). Lyman et al. maintained that women in their study needed more advanced degrees and had to take on more responsibilities than did male principals.

In general, if potential principals receive sincere support from the district office, teachers, and the parent community as they climb the administrative ladder, then the initial period in the principalship is likely to include a broad base of support for one's decisions. This should come as no surprise. Those who promoted your candidacy believe that they can recognize talent. Your success will only affirm their hunch.

Challenges and Problems That Affect All Principals, Both New and Veteran

Some challenges and problems affect all principals—new and veteran. For example, a crisis occurs on campus, or a kindergartner is struck and injured by a car. The success with which the crisis is dealt is a function of several things: a speedy response to the accident enabled by rapid access to emergency numbers and personnel, first aid knowledge, and communication skills to talk with parents, staff members, students, board members, the central office, the police, and the media. There are other challenges, however, that are unique to the newcomer. For instance, many principals new to the job wonder, "Will I have to put my family life on hold?" or "Do others in this role seem as lonely as I do?" Challenges for both rookie and veteran principals in new positions can include the budget process, district-required forms, routines, knowledge of policy, and new school laws.

For example, each state, school district, and individual school has forms and routines that one simply has to learn and use before achieving success in some limited areas. Principals need to know who to go to and how to learn the routines as quickly as possible. Although these might be simple activities for principals familiar with their schools and districts, for the newcomer the activities can be frustrating, time-consuming, and unnerving as one simply wants to get on with the "important" aspects of the job. This is particularly difficult for the principal who is hired from outside the district or state. One state might have a thin manual of state laws and board of education codes, whereas a bordering state might have a collection of codes so extensive that it would take a seventh-century monk a lifetime to interpret and translate them. Is one expected to know every state education code? Of course not, but it is crucial to know how to find out where a code is and who to check with when a further explanation is needed. Initially, finding the right resource (printed or human) to check the accuracy of information can be a very time-consuming activity.

The Importance of the First Year in a New School

About one quarter of a mile from your school is another school with a principal who has been there for 10 years. A newcomer, on the job from the first minute, has just as much official "power" as does the 10-year veteran. You will make decisions—good and bad—that are just as significant as those made by the 10-year veteran. Ironically, as new students, teachers, and parents enter the school, they really do not care about your inexperience in that school; they all want, and deserve, your help and support.

In Charge With Full Responsibility From Day 1

You are expected to provide sagacious advice from the moment you enter the schoolhouse. An effective principal, from the first moment on the job, can make a difference in the lives of numerous students, teachers, parents, and community members. Of course, gaining the same or greater influence, prestige, and trust that the 10-year veteran principal enjoys will take a while, but if you do a good job, you will be surprised at how quickly the school community will support you.

The word "power" was used at the start of this section to describe the official responsibility of the principalship. Today, many specialists on the principalship are uncomfortable with that word. In this book, the word "power" is meant to mean having the authority and resources, and using one's influence, to improve teaching and learning in a school. Quite simply, the principal can have a greater impact on facilitating change, introducing new ideas, helping staff members grow, and influencing instructional and capital resource decisions than can anyone else in the school. One should not assume, however, that it is easy for the principal to implement any of these. Yet, a principal's position of central authority in a schoolhouse certainly makes him or her a key player in all major decisions. Possibly more important, a principal plays a pivotal role in helping to set a moral tone in the school, helping to reduce intimidation and isolation, and increasing trust building and risk taking for both teachers and students.

Interestingly, Gardner (1995), in his book *Leading Minds*, reflects that it is fashionable, on a grand scale, to talk about leaderless movements. However, he maintains that leaderless movements simply do not occur. If one looks at a great historical movement, one will recognize great leaders. This notion is important for the school leader. Do not be shy about your leadership role. Take responsibility and make decisions, but do so in a caring way. Realize the power that sharing leadership and decision making brings. Listen to others, build consensus, support success, and set a personal example by honoring the dignity of each individual in the schoolhouse. It is okay to be a leader and to facilitate the educational discussion based on your pedagogical knowledge. As Joseph Murphy, chairperson of the Interstate School Leaders Licensure Consortium, noted, "There's just overwhelming evidence that [at] the places where things work, the school leaders have a deep understanding of children and learning and achievement" (quoted in Olson, 1996a, p. 5).

As the collaborative decision-making process is employed more frequently as it is in many schools, the principal's role becomes more complex and the demand for specific group decision-making skills is greater. The ability to both inspire and bring closure to discussions, to facilitate abstract ideas becoming concrete ones, and to translate brainstorms into practical action are but some of the competencies to which the newcomer must aspire.

Your First Year Can Be a Predictor of Future Success, So Get It Right the First Time

The relationship between performance during one's first year in a new school and long-term success in that school is an important theme in the literature on the principalship. For instance, Duke et al. (1984) note that "early experience in a position can be a potent shaper of an individual's subsequent performance" (p. 12), whereas Parkay and Hall (1992) theorize that "a principal's eventual level of career development is strongly indicated by the end of the first year" (p. 355). Skelly (1996) cautions principal colleagues, "Be careful! While you may be in your new position for at least several years, much of your success may be determined by how you conduct yourself during the beginning period of your tenure" (p. 90). These notions are both exciting and sobering. Clearly, these ideas suggest that one should not go into the job assuming that one can lead by the seat of one's pants (although there will be such days!) hoping that teachers, parents, and students will be compassionate through a "honeymoon period" of trial and error. Thus, it is imperative to develop successful habits and to foster effective strategies, beginning with the first day on the job. As the principal, you are shaping the organization as the organization is shaping you (Hart, 1993). You do not want to miss the "window of opportunity"—the chance to seize the energy of the newcomer period.

A principal should proactively consider the following important questions. What is the school's mission? How can I positively influence the students? What do I need to do to become an instructional leader or a leader of instructional leaders? What type of impression do I want to make on the community? How should I manage my time so that the teachers see what I believe is important to the success of the school? How can I keep my personal life in order as I become an effective principal?

A new or veteran principal, recognizing the crucial opportunities of the first year in a new school, must ask the question: How can I budget my time to prioritize working with teachers on instructional/curricular issues? This is a critical question. One study of new principals concluded,

The first casualty of a new principalship may be the instructional responsibility of taking the time to visit classes. If one's early actions are a predictor of future actions, it may be difficult for newcomers to reverse patterns that develop early in their principalship. (Alvy & Coladarci, 1985, p. 46)

If principals believe that a major part of instructional leadership is visiting classes, then they must build class visitations into their schedules. Principals who intend to be successful should work to develop, right from the start, productive habits that reveal a *consistency of effective leadership behaviors.*

What is the first impression you want to make on the faculty? How principals conduct themselves during initial faculty meetings might leave long-lasting impressions on the staff. A school principal recently had a former faculty member mention that she still remembered that first faculty meeting in which the principal indicated how much he needed to learn from the teachers regarding teaching, curriculum, and the school. Seven years later, the faculty member reflected on how much that moment meant and how it helped to create fellowship with the staff. That first impression was critical; the trust-building process had begun. That first impression also was to be crucial with students, classified staff, parents, and the community.

Ready to Learn and Ripe for Change

A powerful aspect of the newcomer experience is that one can be more susceptible to changes in one's own behavior during this period. The newcomer often experiences a feeling of vulnerability. Because of this, one often seeks assistance and advice. During this initial induction period, one characteristically is seeking stimulation and learning opportunities and is open to growth.

A principal's voice:

There is a certain freshness and maybe vitality that comes with being new to a place. It's an adventure. There is a certain excitement, and I think that sort of thing carries into a job as well.

Think about when you are in a new situation. As noted earlier, antennas are up, senses are on full alert, and new practices are being established. If the senses are not on full alert, then you will trip over that crack in the sidewalk outside of the school that veteran staff members have walked around for years. (By the way, get that crack fixed, and fix the loose rims on the basketball hoops on the playground, before the school year begins.) Reflect on the practices that you would like to have in place 3 or 4 years later. During the third year in the school, you already will be using "tried-and-true" strategies developed during that first year, so the time to get it right is in the beginning. For example, moving to a new position or school is an opportune time to improve one's time management skills.

One beginning principal began an index card time management system from Day 1. Every time he noted something he wanted to get done, he would write it on an index card. For example, he wanted to change the sign for visitors on the front door of the school to make it more welcoming. Then, whenever he had a spare moment, he took out his card pack and worked on a card that was "doable" in that time frame. Reflecting on this practice, he noted, "It saves a lot of little things from falling through the cracks. Collectively, the little things created the tone, practices, and modeling I wanted to communicate, and it gave me a sense of accomplishment."

When a rookie or veteran principal accepts a school leadership position, he or she can be catapulted into leading immediate change whether the principal is ripe for it or not. If a state or school district mandates a curriculum or policy change, then the newcomer is expected to implement the change. These situations can include times in which many around them do not want the change or do not know what the change is, why it has come about, or how they fit with it. One principal reflected the following after being placed in a school moving from traditional to authentic assessment:

> It's an interesting mix—a time for rapid learning, conflict resolution skills, patience, understanding, empathy, [and] just plain people skills. It's exhilarating, painful, frustrating, complex, and exciting—often all at the same time. You experience a range of emotions as you ride the wave of change.

Admittedly, there are times in which a principal simply wishes there would not be so many changes, such a hectic pace, or such feelings of vulnerability. As one principal noted, "At some times, I just want to stop, or at least slow down, the merry-go-round so I can catch my breath."

CHAPTER 2

The Loneliness
of the Principalship

I felt like I was alone. I couldn't go across and confide with somebody.

A principal's voice

Although the principal interacts with hundreds of individuals on a weekly basis, the principal usually feels isolated and lonely because no one else has the responsibility of the whole school on his or her shoulders. Duke, Isaacson, Sagor, and Schmuck (1984) indicate that the greatest surprises for new principals were "loneliness, time pressures, and unpreparedness" (p. 26). Osterman, Crow, and Rosen's (1993) study of 216 new principals in New York City notes that "one of the major problems confronting new principals is a sense of isolation" (p. 23).

Simply as a result of the traditional school management hierarchy, in most settings, a principal is the only person on site with responsibility for the total program. It is easy to say that in some schools, with the present climate of shared governance, responsibility is disseminated throughout the organization. Reality presents a different scenario. If a child breaks his leg on the playground and a parent thinks the supervision was inadequate, then the parent is *unlikely* to request a meeting of the site council for the following week to register a complaint. (The parent might not even know there *is* a site council.) The parent will want to meet immediately with the principal.

Can the Familiar Be Lonely?

Anthropologist Estelle Fuchs observed that working in a school and teaching there after having been a student can lead to "culture shock" (cited in Ryan & Cooper, 1995). The phrase "shock of the familiar" is used by Ryan and Cooper (pp. 74-75) to describe the experience of new teachers who are not sure how to handle classes, bells, tests, report cards, the food service, and so on even though they were familiar with all these aspects of school culture as students. Individuals, socialized as students, teachers, and likely administrators before becoming principals, also will be familiar with most of the issues with which they deal. Yet, now they are in a position that no one else in the school holds. It might feel great to be the principal, but it also is strange when one realizes that the role will be looked on differently by students, teachers, and parents. The principal is likely the most influential person in the school, and what one has to say takes on increased meaning because of the position. The setting might be familiar, but until one feels familiar in the position and builds up relationships with colleagues, it can be very lonely. Skelly (1996), advising principals, reflects that "friends and colleagues view you differently, and they take your comments more seriously" (p. 90). Moreover, Skelly maintains that the loneliness is compounded if the principal is in a new setting in which he or she does not know anyone. Even the seasoned principal feels lonely when, in a new school across town, he or she reflects at the end of the day "alone again in the principal's office, but how different it is."

Is It Lonelier for the Principal Hired In-District or for the Principal Hired From Outside?

Carlson's research on the superintendency set the stage for examining why districts hire insiders and outsiders and the possible influence that the insiders and outsiders have on the organization (cited in Miklos, 1988, p. 64). Carlson referred to those who are willing to move out of their districts as *career bound,* whereas those who prefer to remain in the district as *place bound* (p. 64).

Miklos (1988) comparing studies of elementary and secondary principal succession, concludes, "The outsiders at both the elementary and secondary levels perceived themselves to have a greater degree of influence with superintendents than did the insiders. Furthermore, the outsider principals were more frequently described by teachers as change agents" (p. 64). Lyman et al. (1993) support this notion in their study of female principals. One district insider noted that "promotion from within the ranks . . . hampered her abilities as a change agent" because she was privy to information that a district outsider would not have had to consider (pp. 31-34).

Should schools hire principals from within or outside of the district? Is it better, or easier, for newly hired principals to be familiar with the norms, values, and faculty of the schools or districts, or are newcomers—and schools—better off with outsiders?

Consider the principal who, as a former teacher, was hired from within a school district. She walks into the faculty lounge a couple of days after the appointment and notices that teachers either pause briefly in their conversation on her entrance or obviously change the topic. It is an unusual feeling, a sudden feeling of alienation for someone who, until recently, was a participant in similar conversations.

Typically, new principals indicate that they used to be the first ones to know about "this or that"; now they are the last ones to find out. Teachers sometimes feel that by becoming a principal, a colleague has "crossed the line" or jumped to "the other side of the fence."

Principals' voices:

I'm just as friendly with them [teachers]. I'm not sure that it is mutual [or] as mutual now as when I was a teacher. As a teacher, you know everything that is going on, and they tell you everything. As an administrator, you're on the other side of the fence, so they don't tell you everything all of the time. (a district insider)

The teachers did not know me, and that's good. (a district outsider)

[There] is a tendency on the part of many of the teachers to want to set up a we-they stance and an adversary role. And I came into this building wanting to be a friend to everybody. I got shot down pretty fast. (another district outsider)

Well, there would be definite advantages to being in-district because you would know the faculty and maybe weaknesses and strengths, [and] you would also know specific curriculum needs. However, I think that to really accomplish [anything], if you're goal oriented, improvement oriented, [and] change oriented, I think that would be very difficult in-district. (a principal echoing Lyman et al.'s [1993] point about change and insiders)

Both insiders and outsiders know that they have not changed, yet others perceive them differently. What has changed? Ironically, even the journals of administrative interns, all insiders completing university certification programs in schools in which they have worked for years, indicate that there is a "distance" from the faculty. The loneliness of the interns was not solely because they were now out of the conversation loop. For instance, one intern stressed a feeling of loneliness not because of social isolation but rather because of the need to preserve confidentiality. "You are privy to information" about students and teachers that cannot be shared (Alvy, 1997, p. 12)

Veteran principals new to districts report that sometimes lack of inside knowledge is a blessing; they might not have to consider a certain amount of information in making a decision or acting. At other times, the same situation can become a curse; they might blunder because of a lack of knowledge about local culture.

The School Culture and Isolation

Can a principal new to a building walk into the hall and ask, "How am I doing?" Most norms of school culture do not permit teachers to ask that question; certainly, a principal cannot. After making a decision, often quickly, a principal might have only a moment, alone and with the door closed, to reflect and consider, "Did I do the right thing?" The next moment, the principal has to open the door and move on to the next thing that comes up.

Newcomer and veteran principals also might feel the loneliness at principalship conferences. Although they know that sharing ideas with others is critical, there might be a fear that others will find out about their "failures."

A principal's voice:

I went to the [state] Principals' Association meeting. But there again, you get the feeling that if you talk to someone there about your problems and they don't know you very well, your problems will be [discussed] all over the state.

Loneliness and the Female Principal

Miklos (1988, pp. 60-61) states that women usually are 5 to 10 years older than men when they become administrators even though women entered teaching at an earlier age. Shakeshaft (1995) notes, "There are more male administrators at every level in schools than there are female administrators" (p. 147). Shakeshaft's analysis stresses that males and females have not been socialized to work together and that we tend to be uncomfortable with a close working relationship. Given that there are more male administrators, it would be reasonable to assume that female loneliness in the job can be greater than that for males. Moreover, Shakeshaft indicated that male superintendents prefer attractive women for elementary school principals, although they are concerned about the complications of working too closely with female administrators as the females move up the administrative ladder. This probably will be the case until the "good ol' girls' club" rivals the size of the "good ol' boys' club."

The loneliness can be accentuated for female principals because they have fewer role models simply due to numbers. A "joke" among females concerning the principals' conference circuit is that females know they are attending a principals' meeting because they never have to wait in line to use a restroom. One female principal noted, "I need to talk with other female principals or teachers just to tell them about how much I miss my kids and how important it is for me to get home in the afternoon."

Another female stated that at conferences or informal meetings,

> When we'd [the principals] go out to lunch, men were always a little bit uncomfortable with me going along because they'd go out for drinks and, you know, talk about something that evidently I shouldn't be included in. I don't know if that was professional respect or what.

Advising and Comforting Others

The loneliness can be accentuated because as newcomers are trying to get their bearings, they are expected to solve the problems of others. By virtue of one's serving in the official position of principal, others assume that there are certain skills and abilities attached to the position whether or not that is the case. The principal might be "learning the ropes," but there is no "do not disturb" sign around his or her neck. People in the building do not hesitate to bring personal and professional problems to the individual in the principal's office. One veteran principal, new to a building, commented, "She came to me to talk about problems at home. I thought to myself, how ironic to do this when I'm trying to get it together here at school myself." Staff members confide marriage difficulties, problems with children, possible career moves, and difficulties with colleagues. These often are not in the job description. Yet, a school principal is expected to have "wisdom."

The cumulative effect of advising and comforting others often is an energy drain. Thoughts that remind the principal of the encounter frequently linger or pop into his or her head later on. This can change one's focus and sometimes can create a sense of fragmentation: "Now, what was I doing?" Many principals have found that getting physical exercise—taking a walk, jogging, or weightlifting—can reenergize and refresh them following emotionally draining encounters.

CHAPTER 3

The Time Juggernaut

In terms of the workload, there are times that I don't feel comfortable. I was here Monday night until midnight after coming at 7 a.m. And then last night, I was here until 2 a.m. after coming at 7 a.m. And I feel real discomfort with that because I feel like if I have to work those kinds of hours to handle the job, then I need some help.

A principal's voice

Peterson (1982) characterizes the principal's day as filled with brevity, fragmentation, and variety. In fact, 85% of a principal's tasks last 9 minutes or less. What is most frustrating to principals is that they seem to have little control over their time or the events, crises, and conflicts that fill up their time. The paragraphs that follow examine several issues related to the time theme and paint a portrait of the principal's day.

The Principal as Juggler:
Role Clarification on the Run

How does a principal manage time when there are so many roles to juggle? How does one keep the balls in the air? Which balls should be dropped or not juggled at all? Consider the various roles that a typical principal handles: advocate for children, instructional leader (i.e., staff evaluator and staff developer), community organizer, pub-

lic relations expert, healer, public speaker, family counselor, media-
tor, emergency school bus driver (without a license), substitute timer
at a basketball game, actor in a school play, volleyball player in the
annual middle school student-faculty game, chaperone at a school
dance, chairperson of the school site counsel, judge at the math-
science exhibition, custodian's helper (e.g., stopping an emergency
leak), staff cheerleader, and morale builder. How does one accomplish everything? What should be the primary role? Is there a primary role? Is role clarification possible? A newcomer might review
the job description and notice that very few of the preceding responsibilities are actually mentioned. One would expect a section devoted
to instructional leadership, responsibility for students, and community public relations within the job description but certainly not actor,
volleyball player, or staff cheerleader.

The staff cheerleading responsibility might seem unimportant or
minor to a principal, but at times that role can be critical and necessary to keep faculty morale high. Personal tragedies can hit a faculty
hard during a year. The principal attends funerals or memorial services when a teacher or student loses a loved one. The principal visits
the hospital to comfort a teacher who suffered a serious accident or
has a serious illness. An administrative intern shared with her university supervisor that she felt that her job was faculty "morale
booster" in a school in which the longtime principal recently had
passed away from cancer. Teachers in the school tried to continue
their teaching as they worked through their grief for a respected and
beloved colleague. In another school, a teacher, leaving the school
after many years, shared with the principal how much it meant to
her that the principal sat with her during an emergency operation of
the teacher's child. That is not in the job description.

Consider the terrible tragedy of TWA Flight 800 and the loss of
the 16 high school students and 5 adult chaperones of Montoursville
High School in Pennsylvania. Anyone who watched on television as
the tragedy unfolded saw how the school principal handled the tragedy with both dignity and grace and helped to rally the community
during the suffering (Gamble, 1996). Every school leader who
watched the principal of Montoursville High must have thought,
"That could have been my school. Would I have maintained such
grace and poise faced with such overwhelming tragedy?" That is not
in the job description.

A teacher going through the tragedy of a parent dying from al-cohol-related illness found it difficult to work as the end was near and shared his grief with the principal. The teacher reflected,

> I told my principal what was going on. He told me to take as much time as I needed and [that] if there was anything he could do, to let him know. Wow, I really needed to hear that. There have been times in my 4 years [at the school] that I have questioned the leadership, but I am beginning to think maybe I was being too judgmental as well as hasty. It is times like these when a principal with compassion really helps.

That is not in the job description.

Feeling Unprepared for the Job

Besides having an expanded "invisible" job description, the principal often feels unprepared for the role despite extensive training. For the newcomer, this easily can lead to a lack-of-confidence crisis. For example, a principal new to a building began the first day of school with the head custodian ill. The calibration system controlling the class period bell was ringing at the wrong time. The new principal felt unprepared: "I don't know how to operate the bell system, yet I have to take responsibility." This is the same principal who, only a few months earlier, was on "cloud nine" and feeling invincible when selected for the job from an applicant pool of about 100 candidates.

Let us take another situation. One principal at the American Embassy School in New Delhi, India, received a frantic call in his office at 7:30 a.m. from a teacher because there was a snake in her classroom. Later the same day, an elephant was on campus. Believe it or not, there were logical explanations for both situations, but getting the right people to handle each situation was not easy. It took time to resolve these unusual events—time that was supposed to be devoted to other responsibilities.

On a more serious note, during the 1991 Gulf War, Saddam Hussein declared that all American institutions were potential terror-ist targets. At the American Embassy School campus, security be-came a major concern. As a preventive measure, the school adminis-tration canceled school buses for 4 months, helped parents arrange car pools, and rerouted campus traffic. Initially, the administration was a bit overwhelmed by the crisis, but with support from the embassy and the parent community, the school remained open without a serious incident. The time juggernaut surfaced during this crisis as the principals served as "campus traffic cops" for several months during the morning arrivals and afternoon dismissals. Meetings about campus security were held almost daily. Obviously, some responsibilities had to be delegated to others or scrapped for several months. Every school, in every community, can provide examples of crises in which one felt unprepared and had to devote extended time to cope with the challenge. Principals need to accept the feeling of unpreparedness as reality and move on to solve challenges as they arise.

Frustration and Surprise
With the Time Constraints

> I learned more and worked harder in my first year than I'd thought possible.
>
> *Daly-Lewis (1987, p. 36)*

Newcomers and veterans often find themselves working long hours to get the job done. One seasoned principal reflected, "I make a "to do" list every morning. Often, when I revisit it at 5 p.m., only one or two items have been accomplished. Things just come up." What happened to the time for jogging, a visit with friends, a good book, or even a professional conference? An important message of this book (emphasized in Part II) is to continue with these healthy activities. Taking care of oneself empowers one to successfully lead and keep things in proper perspective. This is an essential point for school principals because they are such important members of the community in and out of their school buildings.

A principal's voice:

> I've been surprised at the amount of time and weekends that this particular superintendent has asked me to give. . . . It surprises me, and that's the one thing about the job that bothers me.

It is not uncommon for principals to find themselves caught in the middle of not only things that consume time but also the expectation from others that they should work overtime. In some districts, principals talk about unwritten norms implying that the longer hours you work, the better principal you are. Keep in mind that when one creates balance in life, effectiveness usually increases. But admittedly, knowing this does not always take away the inner conflict of "want to's" versus "should's" when it comes to time.

The Time Juggernaut in Action: A Typical Day for a School Principal

The following description provides a serious yet humorous portrait of the school principalship.

The principal, Ms. Walker, wakes at 5:30 a.m. and is ready to leave the house at 6:45 for the half-hour drive to school. Just before leaving, she receives a call from a school secretary letting her know that all three possible chemistry substitute teachers are unavailable today. Ms. Walker remembers that a student teacher is in the chemistry class, so she tells the secretary to get any substitute available. The principal will talk with the student teacher (who will be the actual teacher without pay) about following the lessons plans.

Upon arriving in school, Ms. Walker reviews her scheduled appointments and meetings: two observations with post-observation conferences, a curriculum review meeting, the review of a possible grievance with the union representative, a meeting with three department chairs to go over budgetary proposals for next year, attendance at a musical program, a meeting with five students who will be sharing a multimedia presentation with her, a meeting with parents of a student who might receive a 2-day suspension resulting from a fight, and a scheduled fire drill. Ms. Walker also plans on visiting the lunchroom for about a half hour to talk with students and try to get a feel for student morale. If time permits, she will sit in on the Spirit Week planning meeting with the physical education department at 2:30 p.m. Lunch will have to be sometime on the run.

Ms. Walker catches the chemistry student teacher when he arrives at the school and mentions that they could not get a chemistry substitute but will have a certified teacher in the room. Ms. Walker lets the student teacher know that this is an opportunity and, if things go well, could be a stepping stone to regular subbing after completing the student teaching.

About 10 minutes before classes begin, the secretary lets Ms. Walker know that the main copier is down and the service representative will not be available until tomorrow. The principal calls the guidance office to ask whether other teachers can use that office's copier for the day. The counselors are not very sensitive to the request because this is the third time it has happened in the last month, but they say okay. The custodian, appearing discouraged, drops in to see Ms. Walker to mention some inappropriate graffiti on the walls of the second-floor hallway. The principal accompanies the custodian to the second floor to both show support for the custodian and make a mental note of what was written. She asks the custodian to remove the graffiti as soon as possible.

While returning to her office, a social studies teacher catches Ms. Walker and tells her that he will need to see her today, if possible, about a personal and professional problem. The principal looks at her pocket appointment book and agrees to the meeting and sets it up at the time she was planning to visit the lunchroom; hopefully, there will be a few minutes to spend in the lunchroom following the meeting. Two students, who have been friends for years, stop Ms. Walker to show her the excellent grades they received on their last math test. The grades draw a smile and cheer from the principal. She continues her walk back to the office, picking up a couple of pieces of scrap paper near the trash can and depositing the paper in the can.

Returning to the office, the principal rushes to get her yellow legal pad for the first observation. The class has begun when the principal arrives for the observation. Discretely, she sits in the back. The observation goes well. The teacher, an experienced professional, uses a couple of different questioning techniques during the lesson. Ms. Walker and the teacher have set up the post-observation conference for the next period. They meet in the teacher's classroom. About 10 minutes into the meeting, Ms. Walker is contacted on her two-way radio to come down to the office. Two students had arrived late to a class, and the teacher had refused to accept them in the classroom. A heated verbal exchange had occurred with the teacher, possibly with some profanity. The principal indicates that she will be down in a minute. She apologizes for having to cut short the post-observation conference, asks the teacher to quickly sum up the meeting, and tells the teacher how much she enjoyed the observation experience. As

Ms. Walker leaves the classroom, she asks the teacher to consider working with a couple of first-year teachers as a mentor. They agree to talk later.

Walking down to the office, Ms. Walker has her mind on the possible grievance meeting and parent meeting concerning the soon-to-be-suspended student. The two late comers are outside of the office and a little nervous when the principal appears. This is not the first time they have met. Ms. Walker hears the students out, lets them know they will have early-morning detention for being tardy, and notes that she will follow up on their use of profanity (which they deny) after speaking with the teacher. The students sit outside the principal's office until the next class begins. Ms. Walker asks the secretary to set up a meeting for her, early tomorrow morning, with the teacher involved in the verbal exchange. If possible, Ms. Walker will try to "catch the teacher on the run" sometime today.

Ms. Walker meets with the union representative about the wisdom of asking teachers to attend a future faculty meeting that was not a regularly scheduled meeting as stipulated in the master contract. The principal explains that the meeting will be informational concerning the possible piloting of a new program. They agree that the best strategy is to make the meeting voluntary. After hearing about the pilot program, the union representative mentions that he will encourage staff members to attend and reminds Ms. Walker that the new master contract allows for such discretionary faculty meetings. Following the meeting with the union representative, Ms. Walker reminds herself to carefully review the new master contract. She is pleased with the union representative's support.

Ms. Walker receives an emergency call from the district office to cancel today's fire drill because two schools in the district were given the wrong time and had already held the drill. The superintendent wants to avoid further confusion. Ms. Walker is not too concerned because only the secretaries and custodian knew of the drill. She tells the head secretary and asks her to inform the custodian that the drill is canceled. She is pleased that this is one less activity to worry about today.

Ms. Walker has a few minutes before her parent meeting concerning the student suspension. She decides to walk the halls as students pass between classes. In the halls, she notices that things are going pretty well except for two classes in which students were dismissed very late. They will have trouble getting to their next classes on time.

Several of the late students running down the hall almost knock the principal over—and sincerely apologize. Ms. Walker smiles and excuses the students. She hopes that they do not "read" her response as a sign of weakness. After encouraging a couple of stragglers to get to class, she returns to her office. The parents are waiting, with the father standing up and looking at his watch. The mother is sitting. Ms. Walker smiles, shakes their hands, and asks whether they would like a cup of coffee. The offer of coffee catches the father off guard. Hesitatingly, he says yes to the coffee, as does the mother.

In Ms. Walker's office, the father states that the parents have been "going through hell" and are thoroughly embarrassed by the possibility of a 2-day suspension for their son, especially because Billy never has been in trouble before. Ms. Walker has Billy's file on the desk and a copy of the student handbook, which includes the school's disciplinary policy. She explains that Billy had been in a fight a month ago, and the policy indicates that the consequence of a second violent incident is a 2-day suspension. The parents indicate that they were unaware of Billy's previous trouble and insist on being notified each time a problem occurs. Ms. Walker returns to Billy's file and shows them the notice sent home about the first incident, which explains that a second incident will lead to a suspension. The note is signed by Billy's parents. The parents look at one another; they had never seen the note. The father says that in the future, the school should call them about each incident. The principal indicates that in Billy's case, they will do that because of the forged signatures. She explains that because of previous misunderstandings, the school sends correspondence to parents to obtain parent signatures acknowledging such incidents as documented records of parent contact. All agree that the parents should handle the "forging episode." The parents leave cordially after Ms. Walker indicates that she will notify Billy that the suspension begins tomorrow. He will need to call friends about his homework assignments. Ms. Walker makes a note on her draft of disciplinary procedures for next year to refine the parent correspondence section.

The secretary informs Ms. Walker that she is a few minutes late for the next observation. Because the teacher is new, the principal wanted to arrive as the lesson opened to observe the teacher's initial management techniques. Entering late, Ms. Walker is pleasantly surprised to see each student engaged as the teacher is reviewing math concepts from the previous lesson. The class goes well until the teacher distributes new calculators. The students are unfamiliar with this particular calculator and spend a few minutes "experimenting" with operation possibilities before the teacher can get their attention. It takes about 5 minutes to get the students back on track. The teacher obviously is a bit nervous and frequently glances back toward Ms. Walker, who thinks to herself that she probably would not have had the nerve to introduce and use new calculators during an observation with the principal in the room. Ms. Walker wonders, "Is this a good sign on the part of the teacher—she is willing to take risks? Or, is this a bad sign?" However, after the teacher demonstrates how to use the calculators, the lesson goes well. Ms. Walker is going to meet with the teacher right after class and is pleased because she does not want the newcomer upset by the initial calculator "snafu."

As the period ends and they are about to start the conference, the fire drill bells ring. The secretary forgot to tell the custodian to cancel the drill. Ms. Walker thinks, "What is the superintendent going to say?" She quickly tells the new teacher that she enjoyed the lesson, not to worry about what happened with the calculators, and to re-schedule their conference for tomorrow. If that is not possible, Ms. Walker says to call her at home this evening if she would like to talk about the lesson. She rushes out to see how the drill is proceeding. Her first impression is that all is running smoothly. Following the drill, she receives reports about the drill's effectiveness. The drill was successful except in the band room, where the teacher and students were unable to hear the bells. They left the band room only after seeing other students walking on the school field. Ms. Walker smiles to herself and decides to let the superintendent know that the drill proceeded almost perfectly—even if it was unauthorized.

After assessing the drill, Ms. Walker meets with the teacher who had some personal and professional concerns to share. The teacher, Mr. Globe, lets her know that he cannot get along with the social studies department chair. He has decided to seek a position in an-other school. They discuss the problems. Ms. Walker does not want to lose Mr. Globe because he is an excellent teacher. She tells Mr. Globe that the school cannot afford to lose him. He obviously appre-ciates the positive comments and says he will reconsider after Ms. Walker indicates that she will sit in on a couple of department meet-ings and speak with the chair. Because Ms. Walker has heard similar complaints about the chair from other department members, she re-alizes her conversation with the chair is long overdue. She is a little discouraged because the mental list of things she "should have followed up on" is beginning to get a bit long.

Ms. Walker looks at her watch and sees that she has about 10 minutes left in the period to go to the cafeteria. One of the "privileges" of the principalship is that she can walk into the back room of the cafeteria and grab a sandwich without getting in line. While eating, she talks with several students. This is the best part of her day.

After the quick lunch, Ms. Walker meets with three department chairs to go over proposed budgets for the next year. She is impressed with two of the budget proposals that, although overbudgeted and needing adjustment, are clearly based on proposed curriculum changes and technological needs. On the other hand, the social studies budget indicates a simple 10% increase in texts, consumables, and instructional resources such as maps and globes. The social studies chair proudly states that his decision is based on expected enrollment increases and inflation. Ms. Walker indicates that she will review the proposals. She will then discuss them with the superintendent and the district financial officer. The social studies chair stresses that they have put a lot of effort into these proposals and hope that the school district will not tamper with their work. The chair also indicates that the social studies department is completely behind his budget proposal. As the chairs depart, Ms. Walker thanks them for their efforts.

The musical program already has begun, and Ms. Walker quietly stands in the back of the auditorium to watch. She is amazed at the talent of some of the students and notices a couple of outstanding performances by students who have not done well in their academic classes. After the show, she congratulates the music teacher and the students and rushes to the computer center to see a multimedia presentation by five students. She is pleased by the quality of the presentation and is a little intimidated by the technological sophistication of the students.

On the way back to her office, the custodian stops Ms. Walker to let her know that the second-floor boys' bathroom again is marked with graffiti. The principal accompanies the custodian to the bathroom to see the vandalism (after first making sure that no students are using the facility). She assures him that she will speak in each classroom near the restroom during the opening of school tomorrow and let the students know that anyone caught in this activity might face suspension and definitely will spend time assisting the custodian in keeping the school clean. Ms. Walker looks at her watch and pocket calendar and rushes to the physical education office to listen in and provide moral support for the Spirit Week activities preceding the basketball season. During the meeting, she is pleased to see several academic teachers helping with the planning. She comments that the ideas sound great and that, except for Friday, the Spirit Week activities should not "spill over" into the regular academic classes.

The afternoon dismissal bells ring, and Ms. Walker excuses herself from the meeting to get outside and wish the students a good afternoon while watching how the bus loading is proceeding. After a few minutes, as the last bus is leaving, a parent approaches Ms. Walker. The parent indicates that she heard from her child that some boys are drinking beer at the back of one bus. The principal asks for the bus route and number, thanks the parent, and indicates that she will follow up on the information immediately. Ms. Walker returns to her office, checks the bus driver name list, and calls the central school bus number. She asks that Mr. Smith call her when he finishes his afternoon route. The secretary walks in the office and reminds Ms. Walker about the math curriculum review meeting.

Ms. Walker rushes to the math meeting and notices that elementary, middle, and high school teachers from the district are there along with the curriculum coordinator. This is an exploratory meeting in which the teachers are reviewing the new state math standards and comparing notes on what they think is working and not working with their present programs. The meeting gets a little sticky when the middle school teachers indicate that elementary students are weak on word problems and some aspects of fraction concepts. Ms. Walker silently reflects that the dialogue among the math teachers, stimulated by the standards' movement, probably is more important than any actual content changes in the curriculum.

Ms. Walker leaves the meeting after receiving a call from the secretary that Mr. Smith is on the phone. The principal takes Mr. Smith's call in her office. Mr. Smith, after hearing the rumor from Ms. Walker, provides the names of the students sitting in the back of the bus. He reports that he has observed no unusual behavior. Mr. Smith notes that the child who reported the problem to his parent always sits near the very front of the bus. Ms. Walker firmly asks Mr. Smith to keep an eye on what is taking place in the back and to examine the rear seats at the end of each trip for the next few days to see whether he finds or smells anything unusual. Ms. Walker states that she will ask a faculty member to ride the bus within the next few days or will do so herself. Mr. Smith finishes the call by stating that he never has had a problem on his buses.

Ms. Walker looks at her watch; it is 4:49 p.m. She spends a few minutes examining in-basket items on her desk and places most items into the "circular file." She spends the next hour writing up her notes from the two observations and is pleased that the lessons went well. Ms. Walker places her notes from the new teacher's observation in her attaché case to take home because she expects the teacher to call. She realizes that she forgot to tell the new teacher that principals would be attending a board meeting this evening.

At 6:20 p.m., Ms. Walker leaves the building and notices the chemistry student teacher jogging around the school track. The student teacher waves. The principal shakes her head and wonders where he gets the energy to jog on a school day. The scene of the student teacher jogging remains in her mind as she drives home for a very quick dinner. She decides that she will have to begin some type of exercise program. She makes a mental note to call a health club tomorrow. Traffic is not too bad going home, and Ms. Walker has enough time to microwave the meat loaf dinner she prepared before leaving for school in the morning. Fortunately, she does not have to give a report at tonight's school board meeting, which begins at 8 p.m. While driving back to school, Ms. Walker admonishes herself to remain awake during the board meeting.

CHAPTER 4

Expectations of the Instructional Leader: Promoting Teaching, Learning, and Curriculum Innovation

---

I just didn't get enough in my university supervision class on working with the at-risk teacher.

An assistant principal

Making sure that instructional and curricular goals are addressed is a challenge for all principals. Achieving instructional goals is a major difficulty, in particular, for beginning principals. Parkay, Currie, Rhodes, and Rao (1992) state, "Their responses indicate that today's rookie principals *do* see themselves as providing leadership in their schools' curricular and instructional programs, but a staggering array of problems deter them from devoting continuing attention and energy to the task" (p. 38). This finding is consistent with Osterman, Crow, and Rosen's (1993) study of new principals, which concludes that student achievement and staying abreast of advances in curriculum and instruction were perceived as major difficulties. These conclusions indicate that today's newcomers believe that instructional and curriculum leadership are major responsibilities and that, if they are not immediately successful in these areas, they are somewhat dissatisfied with their own performances.

The Desire to Be an Instructional Leader

When a teacher makes plans to become a principal, the long-range goal is to make a difference in the lives of children. One does not come to this decision lightly. A teacher tends to feel that the classroom is where the action is. It is in the classroom where someone has direct involvement with teaching and learning. A new teacher who, after 2 or 3 years on the job, is advised that "You should think about administration" might be both flattered and bewildered. "Why should I think about administration when I'm just beginning to learn how to teach and instructional leaders are in the classrooms teaching?" To decide to become a principal later in one's career probably includes the thought,

> Yes, I can still make a difference in the lives of children. I can work with teachers, new and veteran, by sharing my experience and helping them to become better teachers through observing their classes, encouraging teacher discussions about teaching, and learning and promoting staff development.

As noted in Chapter 3, you cannot always concentrate on what you know is important. Teachers become principals to be instructional leaders. A teacher who has devoted his or her career to children does not become a principal to be a manager of budgets, instructional supplies, software glitches, and lunch tickets.

Principals' voices:

I came into a situation with no idea what the job was. . . . You know, it's an endless list of things that I was not even aware that a principal ever dealt with. Punching lunch tickets [laugh]—nobody told me that was a biggie.

How do you, in fact, handle angry teachers or the lunchroom? [That] never entered my mind. The chaos that goes on in lunchrooms—what do you do if a school hasn't set up a discipline policy and you come on board?

Instructional Leadership and Visiting Classes

If the newcomer does not make visiting classes a priority, then it might never become one. As already noted, habits often are developed early in one's career, and if classroom visitations are omitted because of "more pressing" responsibilities, then the visits might never occur. In the *Handbook of Research on Educational Administration*, Miklos (1988), reviewing Mascaro's (1973) study of new principals, states that initially a newcomer wants to know what is taking place in classrooms. However, "When principals encounter the problem of insufficient time, the perspective shifted to one of emphasizing brief visits to classrooms, relying on secondary sources of information, and effecting change indirectly" (p. 68).

When teachers indicate that the principal never visits their classrooms, the comments often are interpreted as an indication of relief—for not being "snoopervised." However, principals who make a habit of visiting classrooms, not just for supervising but also to support the classroom experience, send a strong message that they are interested in teaching and learning and that the classroom—not the principal's office—is the center of the school. In addition, visiting classes reminds new principals about the primary responsibility of instructional leadership. Visiting classes should be a priority. As Kent Peterson indicated, "What you pay attention to and spend time on communicates what you value" (personal communication, July 1991). If instructional leadership is valued, then one must ask the question: How should principals behave if they want to be perceived as instructional leaders? Furthermore, visiting classes provides another important avenue for culture building. As the principal moves from class to class, teachers become aware of key values as a consequence of where the focus of each visit is placed. In addition, the principal gathers valuable information about what is going on in the school instructionally.

Broadening One's Scope: Becoming an Advocate for Every Program, Student, and Teacher

In the classroom, you're just concerned with how it affects you.

An intern training for the principalship

One principal formerly served as a teacher, subject area expert, department chair, and advocate for the music program. For 10 years, that teacher lobbied the principal for instructional resources for the music room. Any advocate for a single subject or program, upon becoming a principal, must be an advocate for every subject and program. One's scope must go from a narrow view to a broad view, advocating for each school program. Sometimes a principal can be advocating for a program he or she knows very little about, and the program must receive human, material, and facility improvement because of student needs. Refocusing one's advocacy from a specific concern as a teacher to the broader needs of the school is not easy. Developing a broader perspective is an important step as one becomes socialized as a school principal. That socialization process will be enhanced if the school is viewed as an "ecosystem," recognizing that each program is important and strengthening the collective school community.

The following example illustrates the difficulty of moving from a narrow view to a broad view.

A former social studies teacher and high school principal was selected as a new elementary principal. Upon becoming the elementary principal, the newcomer saw almost everything through the eyes of a social studies teacher and high school principal. When he looked at funding for the next year, he thought of globes, maps, social studies texts, multimedia simulations of the American West, and CD-ROMs on historical themes or geographic features. The principal read and was quite impressed, reluctantly, with the 1989 National Council of Teachers of Mathematics (NCTM) standards. The newcomer initially resented the document because the social studies standards (e.g., geography or history standards) had not led the way. The NCTM document had become the trailblazing standards movement document. In fact, when studies indicated that students were bored in social studies classes, the principal tended to ignore the data because he was convinced that social studies was the most interesting curriculum area in need of the least tinkering. Many principals begin the job with particular experiences, certain interests, and unique vantage points. Socializing oneself to a broader view and learning about the other disciplines is a real challenge.

A principal's voice:

There is a tendency, and I went through it myself, for teachers to feel that administrators forget that they were teachers once, too. I don't think that's the case. I think that once you start operating from a different frame in the system, your outlook changes from single program to total program, and that causes some real problems.

Interestingly, in the preceding quote, the principal indicated that the perception of a teacher is that principals forget that they were once teachers. The implication is that the principal is now insensitive to the particular or unique needs of a specific teacher or department. This can be a very touchy development for the newcomer, who might now be perceived by his or her former colleagues in the science department as abandoning their needs in favor of English or physical education.

Broadening one's scope also relates to moving from the classroom, which is perceived as a teacher's territory and (as noted earlier) often an isolated setting, to an administrative office, which should be open to all staff members. Using the classroom mind-set, the new principal needs to be careful about thinking that the office is the territorial area of the principal, secretary, and only a few trusted advisers.

The Difficulty of Providing Assistance to the Marginal Teacher

A principal's voice:

So, I had two shots at evaluation workshops, and I felt like that wasn't enough. When it comes time to write improvement plans for teachers and talk about what they can do to improve their teaching, I felt that was one part of the evaluation training that I did not get.

Another problem for new principals, and for veteran principals assigned to new buildings, is working with teachers who clearly need to be on assistance plans to improve their skills. Some teachers who need to be on assistance plans will simply resist the best efforts of principals and teaching colleagues to help them. They often will resort to the union for protection, and it is the union's responsibility to support all teachers, even those who are not interested in change.

A considerable amount of time is needed to work with teachers who need to be on assistance plans. If a teacher's dismissal is the district objective, then the documentation and paper trail can take more than 80% of a principal's time over several months and cut considerably into the instructional supervision of other teachers. Battling the firing of a teacher can cost a school district more than $80,000 in legal fees and other expenses (Johnson & Lombard, 1996). A lot of principals feel that it is just not worth the effort. A principal new to a school wants to first establish himself or herself. To take on a veteran teacher who needs help can be very risky. Unquestionably, if dismissal is necessary, it must take place. However, it is emotionally difficult and traumatic for all involved, and the process can sour one's desire to help others improve their skills.

Graduate training provides students with a course in supervision. However, graduate students usually want specific information on how to assist marginal teachers. They already have heard that assisting the marginal teacher is an emotional, time-draining experience for everyone. The dilemma is that too much discussion during training on strategies for marginal teachers might leave graduate students with the impression that one should focus all of his or her efforts on this small minority and "firing" teachers. Most training programs instead focus on supervision, staff development, and differentiated professional growth options for *all* teachers. Consequently, principals often feel inadequate about working with marginal teachers.

How Do You Provide Differentiated Professional Growth Options When You Do Not Know the Faculty?

Another instructional problem for new principals in a building is that until they have an opportunity to see everyone teach and find out about faculty interests, it is difficult to facilitate professional growth. Most states and districts have some type of evaluation plan in effect. For untenured teachers, a standard evaluation form usually is designed with clear time lines and minimum observation hours expected by the principal. For tenured, more experienced teachers, development plans allow for professional growth options that range from taking additional courses/credit hours/workshops during the year or summer, to mentoring new teachers, peer coaching, developing grants, presenting workshops, developing innovative curricular or teaching possibilities, or serving on instructional, curriculum, or site council committees.

It can be difficult for a principal to endorse a growth plan that a teacher is enthusiastic about until the principal knows the teacher's strengths and areas in need of improvement. Conducting management by wandering around visits to classrooms can provide an initial awareness of teachers' instructional skills and curriculum coverage. Although this does not replace the value of an extended observation, it can provide an initial starting point for dialoguing about the teacher's professional growth plan. Sometimes during one's initial year on campus, that is the best one can do.

Developing an Instructional Vision

In addition to working with individual teachers, the principal new to a site needs to develop a greater understanding of a collective schoolwide instructional vision. Again, this will take time. The school likely already has a vision or mission statement that describes what the school aims to promote regarding teaching, learning, and building. But is the vision a reality? Often a newcomer finds out that what is written in the vision, mission, or philosophy statement does not really take place on a day-to-day basis. One useful strategy is to invite teachers to revisit the vision, compare it to data regarding "what is," and identify subsequent steps. Facilitating this process demonstrates the value that one places on working toward a vision. Many newcomers feel a need to make their instructional mark on the school early and will struggle with what that mark should be.

Changing the Traditional Master Schedule

In many middle and high schools, a virtual revolution is taking place regarding the student master schedule. The traditional 45- to 55-minute class period is being replaced by 80-minute block scheduling, rotating schedules, and other innovations to improve teaching and learning (Canady & Rettig, 1995). Elementary schools, moving away from traditional scheduling and tracking, are moving toward ungraded classes, combination classes, and year-round schooling.

Where does this leave principals who take over schools that are still very traditional? As will be discussed in the next chapter, a principal usually does not come into a school and immediately change the system. Quick change often is a formula for disaster. Newcomers want to make significant instructional changes but initially might move slowly until the school culture is assessed and enough credibility is earned to successfully implement changes and improve instructional programs.

A master schedule, traditional or restructured, is not just movable pieces on a magnetic board or software for a computer program. Each scheduling decision represents a teacher, with strengths and weaknesses, who is guided by the schedule and students who need to be placed in classes that will address their needs. Maximizing the talents of each teacher and creating educational opportunities for students through the schedule is a major instructional task. Learning about the strengths of each teacher, the best subject assignments, various scheduling possibilities, student needs, and how to implement the changes thoughtfully takes time.

What is critical is that, ultimately, a schedule selected reflects the needs and desires of staff members, students, and parents. There is a temptation to select a schedule because of its popular use in other schools. Doing so in the absence of data about faculty members, students, curriculum, special programs, and other factors unique to a school might spell disaster. There must be a reason to change a schedule, not just because it is the thing to do. Fortunately, for a principal new to a school, developing a schedule for the following year usually does not become an issue for consideration until about mid-year. By that time, the principal should have considerable data about the school to make good scheduling decisions with colleagues. A helpful matrix for making effective choices about scheduling options will be described in Chapter 13.

CHAPTER 5

The Complexity of Relationships: Faculty, Students, Classified Staff, Parents, and the Community

I would like more [staff contact] because I respect them so much for the job that they're doing. I think that professional contact with them is important. And there are times that they've been frustrated because they can't get in to see me because I've been working with kids, or I've had meetings to go to, or I was passing the bond issue and doing presentations. And I feel like the time constraints have caused me to have less contact with them than I would like to. . . . For example, in terms of evaluation, I feel like every time I observe, I should have a conference immediately after the observation, and I was not always able to do that.

A principal's voice

A key leadership issue in the principalship is developing strong and healthy relationships. Principals interact with people all day—teachers, students, classified staff, parents, and the community. Usually, when someone needs to see a principal, there is something wrong or a quick decision needs to be made. Developing the skills to cope with these challenges is not easy, especially because quality reflective time to make good decisions usually is at a minimum.

Faculty Relationships

Teacher interactions with principals vary and can relate to staff assignments, coping with a particular student, planning an event, supervision of instruction, budget requests, a personnel conflict, an abusive parent, or a request for a personal day. Interestingly, new or seasoned principals quickly learn that some faculty members believe that the principal has unique skills as a counselor and will be expected to resolve sensitive and personal family or community issues.

A major concern for all principals is the value of developing a strong positive relationship with the faculty. They want to become part of the system and part of the culture of the school. When the newcomer finds himself or herself in a new school and community, relationships seem even more important. It can be very difficult to develop a network of faculty colleagues because the person in the principal's office no longer is one of the "teacher gang." All principals, both new and veteran, value positive relationships with faculty members, perhaps because of the loneliness of the job and the influence that relationships have on the decision-making process in a school.

Relations With the Veteran Staff

A principal's voice:

Old guard teachers—experienced teachers—resent anyone taking a strong leadership role with them. They feel that they should be able to run the school and make the decisions.

Relations with veteran staff can be an especially tricky issue if one or more of the veteran teachers had applied for the principalship and did not get the job. For example, in one very small school, 4 of the 16 teachers applied for the principalship. The school district hired an outsider for the job. Working with the veteran staff in this situation was very problematic for the principal, but eventually she succeeded.

One experience that can be unnerving for a principal new to a school is having the experienced teachers and classified staff always telling the newcomer how to do things. It is tough because the principal often believes that he or she is the one who is supposed to know how things work. Newcomers have to be very careful and not permit their egos and lack of confidence to take over to the point at which they are giving advice or directions about subjects they know little about. This can easily happen if a newcomer seeks to display confidence and project an image that "I know what I am doing." It is an easy trap for a principal. The pressure to "know" when one does not know is not easy to overcome, as one newcomer discovered.

A principal's voice:

At the beginning, [an understanding of the school was] pretty tenuous. [It is] pretty good now. They [veteran teachers] understand because I'm experienced now. I've been here almost a year. I've made the mistakes. I've failed. I've succeeded. [I've] done both. So, I think it's pretty good now. I think for a first-year principal it's tough. [It's] really tough because they know more than you. Let's be honest. Even though you've got a degree, even if you've been a principal. Let's say you've been a principal somewhere else. They know more than you. They know the way things go, so it's tough.

Gaining Credibility With the Veteran Staff

If word has trickled down that you were a good teacher, an exceptional assistant principal, or a successful veteran principal, then that should help build credibility with veteran teachers. However, one cannot always rely on the rumor mill to provide such a convenience.

A principal's voice:

I'm probably one of those fortunate individuals because of [my] having over 20 years in the classroom. They get the feeling this guy's a teacher as well, and he has been around . . . so I think we've got a great relationship going.

Principals know that to succeed, they must work with the seasoned veterans. Yet, knowing what they should do and actually accomplishing those objectives might not be all that easy, as one principal noted.

A principal's voice:

Certainly I can say, off the top of my head, that you should involve these people [veteran teachers], give them some responsibility, make them feel like they're leaders in the school. Those are all the things we hear and we know. But, saying that and actually doing it, and pulling it off, without them saying, "We're being had, . . . we're not going to do it, we don't want to do it"—this kind of thing, it's more difficult than it sounds.

This reflection raises the very interesting issue of *manipulation*. Principals know that they should work with veteran staff members and that to succeed in the school they must have them on the team. Yet, principals need to involve faculty in an honest way, developing relationships sincerely. Sometimes new principals encounter considerable opposition from veteran faculty members and experience difficulty becoming "insiders." Confronting obstacles (some expected and others unexpected) during the transition from the encounter stage to the insider stage is a natural phenomenon. As one develops relationships and learns the norms of the schoolhouse, he or she experiences gradual inclusion. Daresh (1993) notes that even if the previous principals were inadequate, they often are missed: "Their teaching staffs often acted as if the former principal were still working in their buildings" (p. 4). Daresh also stresses that "grieving" the loss of the previous principal is simply reality and that newcomers should accept this fact as a natural event (p. 11). Loss of the familiar often generates feelings of vulnerability among those left behind. Principals who succeed recognize this and frequently spend time "taking stock" of the situation, context, and players before acting.

In addition, a principal new to a building often encounters jealousies that develop if teachers feel the newcomer is showing favoritism toward certain teachers. Delegating is very important, especially when site-based decision making is so often a common practice at school sites. Principals want to quickly find out who talented members of the staff are and whether they are willing to spend time in a shared leadership role. If it is perceived by the principal new to the site that one of the key teachers is a relatively new member of the staff, then one might need to plan proactively how this will be received by the faculty, especially the veterans. After all, a highly skilled teacher who also is relatively new to a building might encounter jealousy and grief from veteran colleagues simply because it goes against the grain of "the way business has always been conducted" at the school. Traditions tend to be sacred and protected. If you want to know about reading, you go to Mr. Jones. If you want to know about science, you go to Ms. Rojas. All music programs must first be approved by Mr. Andrews. It takes time for all new staff members to identify the cultural icons and traditions of the school.

Introducing Change With the Staff

> An assumption underlying the research on administrative succession is that a change of administration is a significant event in the history of an organization.
>
> *Miklos (1988, p. 63)*

A principal's voice:

I don't think you can be real hard-nosed toward the teachers that first year. They are really going to resent you anyhow because they were familiar with the person before you, and the way things have been flowing. I kind of think you should pretty much go along with the system the first year.

The Difficulty of Creating a Vision

In Parkay and Hall's (1992) study of new principals, Roberts and Wright (1992) note that a few new principals try to implement immediate changes with regard to "managing student conduct, improving school climate, and improving instruction" (p. 130). The researchers suggest that the new principals showed an increasing concern for school climate and a *developing vision* as the year progressed. It seems logical that new principals would concentrate their efforts on issues related to climate and vision once they believed that they had learned the managerial aspects of their positions and that the operations were running smoothly.

On the other hand, Roberts and Wright (1992) report that change efforts of any type were not attempted by a significant number of the beginning high school principals in the study. Curiously, Parkay and Hall (1992, p. 355) report that by their third year, the new principals recognized that their early visions or expectations for change were "unrealistic."

Unrealistic expectations and visions often result from principals acting the role they believe they should play. When this happens, their "human side" often is submerged beneath the role. As a consequence, principals new to school buildings might experience resistance and skepticism from the staff. Reflecting on the first-year experience, one newcomer shared the following.

A principal's voice:

I acted how I thought principals should behave, not how I wanted to in my heart of hearts. In retrospect, following the adage "to thine own self be true" would have been better. I did this later in the role and was more successful.

Shaping the Organization

New principals, by their very presence, represent change and, as noted in Chapter 1, are shaping the organizations at the same time as the organizations are shaping them (Hart, 1993). According to Hart (1993), the principal is "shaped by the social forces around [him or] her and through which [his or] her self-awareness emerges" (p. 10). Experienced teachers have worked years building relationships with former principals, and the question occurs to everyone, "What will the new principal think of me? I know I'm an excellent teacher, and our last principal knew it, but will the new principal think I'm a good teacher?" Hart reminded us that teachers, district supervisors, and the new principals themselves all encounter "apprehension and fear of the unknown with high expectations being held" for the new principals' successes (pp. 6-7).

School boards often bring principals in to facilitate changes they want to see accomplished. Although principals might know that change can bring loss and insecurity to a faculty, that change is a process, that change takes place one person at a time, and that things might get worse before they get better during change (Deal, 1985; Fullan & Stiegelbauer, 1991), when reality hits the literature does not provide a sense of comfort. The newcomers might have been selected because of past performance, sticking to the program, working with the establishment, taking the state courses for certification, and having been conditioned as school persons their whole lives, but when "the rubber meets the road," change might be extremely difficult to implement.

Sources of Assistance

Parkay, Currie, Rhodes, and Rao (1992) suggest that, in general, principals learn to cope with very little help. For new principals, the district, principal peers, and faculty/staff, lead the way in providing support. Part of successfully completing the socialization process for principals is receiving increased assistance from the faculty. As this occurs, the players in the school culture become more collaborative.

Who the principal chooses as a source of assistance also depends on the size of the district. In New York City, principals have little contact with the district superintendent or the school chancellor. On the other hand, in Lincoln, Montana, the principal will interact with the superintendent every day. In a large elementary, middle, or high school, the veteran assistant principal might be a key source of help to the newcomer. Of course, if the assistant principal applied for the principalship and was not selected for the job, the relationship could be difficult at first; in fact, it could be difficult for years. When accepting a position, it always is helpful to ascertain what the circumstances were surrounding the selection process to determine the dynamics of one's appointment. It simply provides for another source of "proactiveness" when contemplating actions.

Hopefully, as a principal develops relationships with teachers, these will become the primary source of assistance for the newcomer. Also, as one becomes a veteran principal and has attended several principal conferences, peers will become a great source of assistance. Some female principals have reflected that it might be a little tougher for females simply because they are a minority within the administrative "club." As the number of female principals increases, this source of assistance also will increase.

Student Relations

A principal's voice:

I miss the classroom. I love the teaching. The counseling—I still have the opportunity to do that, whether it is with parents, or kids who are in trouble, or teachers who are upset. That's always there. But the teacher role is not there as often as I would like it to be.

We are educators primarily because we enjoy interacting with young people. For many principals, "distancing" themselves from students can be one of the most disturbing parts of the job. Indeed, a principal's role in supervising the behavioral program in a school can create and intensify a barrier with students. Although in many larger schools, "discipline" is handled primarily by an assistant or vice principal, the principal ultimately is responsible for all decisions and still is perceived as the "heavy." It is both humorous and sad that when parents first meet a principal, they often state with a smile, "It's nice meeting you, but I hope our child doesn't have to spend any time in your office." One of the most difficult, complex, and frustrating aspects of the principalship is balancing the need to develop meaningful *individual* relationships with students with the firmness necessary to create a safe and orderly environment for the *whole* student body.

Projecting a Firm Image

A new high school principal recalled his first days on the job when he was obsessed with catching students smoking in a restricted "no smoking" area. The principal felt that he had to "apprehend" the students right away to prove he could "catch kids," solve the smoking problem, and handle disciplinary responsibilities. The pressure to look good—like an enforcer—in front of the kids, parents, and (most important) teachers meant a great deal to this newcomer. But 2 or 3 years later, he could not even remember the specific students involved in the incident. Experience certainly helps one get a better perspective concerning the magnitude of a disciplinary problem and how much time and energy one should spend on particular incidents.

Managing student behavior in many schools has become one of the most complex aspects of the principalship. The severity of incidents has caught our whole society by surprise, and not just in urban areas and high schools. As a case in point, in February 1996, a middle school student walked into his math class and shot and killed his teacher and two classmates while injuring others and holding students hostage until a physical education teacher forced the student into surrendering. The town in which this tragedy occurred, Moses Lake, Washington, is a typical small American city. The school district of Moses Lake responded as any other city would. It reexamined security policies, emergency response procedures, guidance program, role of parents, and student relationships and considered what the community could do in the future. It would be easy to state that this is an extreme example, but it is not. Schools must hope for the best but be prepared for the worst.

Rookie and seasoned principals new to school buildings, like new teachers, have to establish themselves. To "test" a principal, students might push the limits about smoking rules, closed campuses, security exits, proper identification, weapons, abuse of teachers, use of illegal drugs, vandalism, and/or cheating. This is not new. What is new is the severity and frequency of the disciplinary incidents.

Becoming familiar with the culture of a school and which rules are critical is not easy. Finding out which teachers are respected by students, and which teachers send students to the principal or assistant principal for minor offenses, takes time. Most important, maintaining or establishing a nonintimidating, welcoming atmosphere in a school is one of a new principal's primary objectives. It takes time to establish oneself and project a firm but caring image with the students.

Curiously, a school's student behavior program frequently is reviewed in administrative textbooks as a management or organizational responsibility. A firm approach to student behavior might be perceived as a "making the school more efficient" issue. However, encouraging appropriate student behavior might be the most complex relationship issue that a principal faces. Discipline is not just getting the operation in order. It should be a teaching and counseling opportunity. This can be particularly complex for the student whose parents have one code of conduct (e.g., "If anyone hits you, hit him harder so he'll never forget you") and the school has another.

Again, conceptualizing the school as an ecosystem is relevant here. Inappropriate behavior can be caused by almost any aspect of a student's life in or out of school. Disciplinary problems can be caused by the climate of the school, repressive school policies, family issues, community problems, and low expectations for students by administrators, teachers, and parents. A principal needs to carefully consider all the possibilities when assessing how a school handles discipline.

Conflicting Interests: The Individual Student and the Needs of the School Community

The principal also has a moral obligation to consider the rights of each student and a community of students. This is an overwhelming responsibility, one that sometimes "exposes" a principal to conflicting values and objectives. On the one hand, a principal needs to consider doing what is best for each student. On the other hand, a principal needs to consider what is best for the school as a whole. This is the same dilemma that each classroom teacher faces, but for the principal the conflict is on a larger scale. Not only does the principal have to consider the individual student and the collective student community, he or she also must consider how the decision will be received by the individual teacher, the faculty, the individual parent, and the parent community—all of whom may have different views on discipline.

Developing a broader view and considering what is best for the whole community—in a sense, diminishing the needs of the individual—can be a particularly agonizing process for a principal. For example, a principal, in conferring with the student newspaper faculty adviser, might decide that a student poem proposed for the student newspaper includes language and content inappropriate for a high school newspaper. Unfortunately, the proposed poem might have been written by a student who, until recently, showed no interest in any school activity. Moreover, the student's participation in the newspaper seemed to have a positive affect on his general school performance. The student threatened to quit the newspaper if his poem was rejected. Although the principal wants the student to continue working on the student newspaper, the decision to reject publication of the poem rests on the need to maintain moral and ethical literary standards for the community of students.

Another dilemma that principals face regarding the needs of a small minority, as opposed to the general student community, relates to one's advocacy of a school program with limited or selected enrollment. To illustrate, a principal might have to decide whether to support funding for a "gifted" program that affects only 5% of the students or to support funding for a series of special events assembly presentations that address the needs of all the students.

The Desire to Remain Close to Students

The loneliness of the principalship is not just a phenomenon that one experiences with teachers. A principal also can feel distant from students.

A principal's voice:

You're different. You are looked at a lot different. You know [that] there's suddenly with the principal . . . all sorts of assumptions. Kids have this feeling about you. Deep down, they respect and like you, but there is a feeling, the principal is—god dang it, he's the principal. He's the S.O.B. of the school. He has got to be, that's his job.

Principals might want to shout, "I am the same person. I still care about students, and I am not just concerned with student discipline." But students, teachers, and parents do not perceive them the same. A principal was told by a resource room teacher that one afternoon, following the principal's visit to the class, a student remarked, "The principal said hello to me and knew my name." It surprised the child and made the child's day. Yet, why should this surprise the student, and why should a teacher feel that it was important enough to share with the principal? It is because, to some extent, we are trapped by our traditional view of the principal as an authoritarian, disciplinary figure—a figure who can be distant from students.

Interestingly, some individuals will be uncomfortable with a principal who does not embrace the traditional authoritarian role. It is hard work for principals to break out of this traditional orientation. Principals must recognize that most students, teachers, and parents will embrace the traditional view of the principalship until they see the principals behave differently. It might be a very slow process, but it is critical in the early days of leadership to display the attributes of the caring professional considering that first impressions are so lasting.

Working With the Classified Staff

A principal's voice:

I've been astonished at the emotional quality of that secretary and my staff and the volatile reaction. And so, I have learned to deal with them in a much different manner than I have been dealt with in former educational experiences.

Classified staff members, all of the noncertificated employees in the school, can positively or negatively affect the success of the student program. In conceptualizing the school as an ecosystem, it is important to realize that every individual and organizational component can help to contribute to student and adult success. For example, the school secretary (e.g., principal's secretary, administrative assistant, attendance secretary, assistant secretary) is the first person encountered by most individuals who contact a school. What type of impression will the secretary make? And the custodian—what about the condition of the school grounds, the hallways, the bathrooms, the gymnasiums, the laboratories, the theater, and the cafeteria? In addition, keeping the equipment safe in a school playground is a paramount concern for a conscientious custodian. Is the school attractive and clean?

Many principals have laughed and then said in a serious tone that secretaries run the schools. Initially, this might not be too far from the truth, especially for principals hired from outside of the district (Alvy, 1983). Newcomers to the district, unfamiliar with the school culture, will depend on their secretaries and ask them hundreds of questions. This makes sense considering that outsiders know much less about "how things" work around their buildings. A very sensitive and difficult issue relates to the desire to maintain the importance of the secretary without the secretary imposing his or her vision of the school—especially if the vision is self-serving. A newcomer has to have enough confidence to balance a desire to implement new systems with the need to depend on the secretary, who might be training the principal in the old systems.

The outside world sees the school secretary as working primarily with the principal. But inside of a school, we know that a first-rate secretary can make life a lot easier for teachers, positively affecting teacher morale. The effective secretary makes sure that the copier gets fixed by calling the service company (or, preferably, she knows more about the copier than does the service employee). A good secretary knows the best substitute teachers (and convinces them to work when they have other plans), serves as a substitute nurse, and provides a welcome shoulder for a student, parent, teacher, or new principal. For the new principal, the potential positive role of the secretary can be offset if the relationship is strained. If a secretary had a strong loyalty to the previous principal, then it can be tough to hear, "This is the way Ms. Perfect did it." This can be very tricky for the newcomer, who was brought in specifically to do it differently than Ms. Perfect did it.

In a very direct way, the skills of the food service manager in the cafeteria affect the well-being of the students. For some students, the school meals might be the only opportunity for nutritious food during the week. Everyone likes good food and a little creativity in the cafeteria; food does not have to taste "institutional." There is a lot of pressure on a staff that is preparing food for hundreds, and sometimes thousands, of individuals each day. Recognizing and supporting the role of the food service staff is an opportunity for a school principal. A principal can exercise that role by ensuring that students are respectful of cafeteria workers and the facility. A clean cafeteria can be a symbol of school pride. And it works both ways. As a consequence of the courtesy extended, cafeteria workers might go out of their way to cater a special meeting or parent group function.

Parents and the Community

One of the great difficulties for all principals is balancing the needs of the students with all the various constituent parent interests. A principal new to a school faces the problem of alienating parent groups almost before he or she begins by taking a seemingly innocuous position on an issue. For example, the principal might suggest that the school should spend more money on technology. As a result, he or she might have a little difficulty with the parent group that feels that more resource money should be devoted to the arts, football helmets, the music program, or classical books. Should the principal tiptoe around issues and remain on the margin initially to develop credibility in the community as someone who keeps an open mind? Of course, trying to remain on the margin for a while also can be perceived as being unprincipled. Some parents might express their frustration by stating, "Doesn't that principal stand for anything?"

Someone who is familiar with the district, a district insider, might have an edge here.

A principal's voice:

I felt very comfortable with the knowledge of the system. But maybe you tend to draw on experiences and not look for different ways of doing things. . . . I think it's nice to be able to know your community, know what you're drawing, and be able to have that advantage. For my purposes, I thought it was fine that I went through the system.

Finally, the most difficult interactions with parents relate to problems with their children. Initially, the new principal can be at a disadvantage if not hired from that school because he or she does not know the history of those children, their families, or their teachers. (The new principal's refrain, "I'm new to this school," might work for a while.) Of course, a lot depends on the size of the school; the larger middle and high schools will have an assistant principal handling most of the disciplinary problems (more on that later).

Another challenge for a new principal is discovering which individual parents and parent constituencies are the community power brokers. Sometime during the principal's career, he or she might have to buck the power brokers and risk the consequences to implement programs to improve teaching and learning. Developing trustful relationships with the power brokers can be very helpful when the difficult times occur.

A principal's voice:

When I came here, they had kind of a businessmen's club which involves a lot of . . . the big wheels in the community. You get in

with them and you know pretty much how the world turns as far
as the town goes.

Ideally, one hopes that the newcomer will have that honeymoon
period with the community, parents, staff, and students that one
hears about (does it really exist?). Unfortunately, with a group that
has a particular agenda, a principal can be trapped in the fray almost
immediately. For example, the principal needs to discern whether a
new disciplinary policy has been instituted recently. Is the principal
going to have to test "the disciplinary experiment?" Is the school
battling the issue of creationism and evolution? Teaching about
AIDS? Reducing varsity sports? Increasing varsity sports? Censor-
ship in the library? A backlash to technology?

A serious risk and problem would be to go along with the community flow even if it means sacrificing what is important and what
one might feel is critical to teaching and learning. It is unfortunate to
hear a principal say the following in relation to adopting the community values and ideas.

A principal's voice:

We all have to prostitute ourselves in some way.

For a principal, the idea of being dismissed following the first
year in a new school is not a welcome thought. However, we all worry
about failure. A newcomer might pursue the following logic very
innocently: "After I solidify my position, I can make the changes that
are necessary. I just need to go along with the program for a while."
The risk of sacrificing what you believe in is a very real thought.
Again, if the first year is a predictor of future success, then what about
your educational vision? How does your vision align with the community and staff values? It can be dangerous to give up that vision
before it is refined.

Principals were teachers, and before that they were students.
They have been socialized all their lives to work in schools and to
learn school values. It probably is not too much of a stretch to expect
that a principal will assume the values of a school community (they
are likely already our values). One might not even realize what is
taking place.

A principal's voice:

I've found that I've assumed some of their values almost un-knowingly.

The Complexity of Site-Based
Decision Making and Site-Based Councils

Site-based decision making, also referred to as site-based manage-ment teams, school improvement teams, and advisory councils, is based on the premise that those who are most affected by educational decisions should be actively involved in the decision-making pro-cess. A major surprise for the newcomer can be finding out that he or she is the leader and is accountable for all major decisions concerning faculty, classified staff, curriculum and instruction, students, fiscal, and facility issues, yet the newcomer must *collaborate* on many of these decisions with a council. Site-based decision making has placed principals in the position of working with teams of adults to make collaborative decisions yet personally biting the bullet when some-thing goes wrong.

Interestingly, in many ways every principal is new to this issue and the many questions to be answered concerning site-based leader-ship. These questions and issues include the following. Who is on the council? How is it governed? What aspects of the school program are within the council's responsibilities (e.g., curriculum, hiring, budg-eting, after-school activities, facility use)? These questions need to be addressed in a charter with bylaws developed for the site council. Other charter issues include the mission of the school, how authority is vested in the council (i.e., state laws or informal), length of mem-bers' appointments, whether the council is ad hoc or permanent, meeting dates, how information will be provided about issues, solic-iting community input and feedback, voting procedures, and defin-ing consensus.

The site council frequently includes all the diverse groups in a school including administrators, teachers, classified staff, students, parents, and community members. The actual and perceived inter-ests of each group might not align with the school's mission. Conse-quently, group decision-making skills and facilitating group interaction have become critical to the principalship. Tools to create win-win situations need to be acquired and practiced.

As noted, although the principal might have a site council that is involved in shared decision making, he or she should assume that when something goes wrong, parents are not going to ask that the site council convene. They will look for the principal based on tradition and convenience. According to site-based theory, responsibility is distributed; reality might be quite different.

Many school leaders have gingerly approached site-based management because the jury is still out concerning whether the process positively affects student achievement. James Esposito, of the University of Virginia, conducted a study looking at site-based decision making involving teachers and indicated that "there is no evidence that it [site-based management] has anything to do with student achievement as measured by standardized tests" (quoted in Lawton, 1996, p. 7). Observers of site-based schools maintain that site-based councils will likely have little effect without a school's commitment to quality teaching and learning; it is a "chicken or the egg" situation. If the decision-making process is inclusive but hollow on teaching quality, then site-based management is not likely to help students (p. 7).

Finally, although site-based decision making might have complicated the principal's role, many practitioners support the more inclusive decision-making process. Nancy Earl, a principal in Manassas, Virginia, prefers site councils because the school can reach out to parents, reduce financial waste, and exercise greater input in how district moneys are spent. "Now the principal has more control, especially over finances. And the school staff and the community are able to direct the finances toward what is needed for that school" (quoted in Olson, 1996b, p. 9). Earl, however, recognizes that juggling the many roles of the principalship has become more complicated in this site-based era because she must use a more collaborative leadership model and serve as a "community liaison, instructional leader, and chief financial officer" (p. 9).

CHAPTER 6

Management Concerns

When considering a principal's responsibilities in the management arena, one should not be surprised that rookie and veteran principals new to their buildings experience feelings of unpreparedness. A principal must become efficient in the management areas relating to policies, procedures, rules and regulations, school records, finances, the master contract and grievance procedures, the school facility, and operating the school within the limits of the law. In many cases, a newcomer learned about school law only recently (and now has to implement the law), is just learning the district budgetary procedures, is unfamiliar with the "nooks and crannies" of the school facility, and immediately needs to learn how to use the district software program on student scheduling, grading, and personal information. These management responsibilities often take time away from instructional leadership endeavors. Yet, if they are not taken care of, they might impinge on the instructional program. "Walking the tightrope" and maintaining a sense of balance in both areas of responsibility is important. Some principals artfully combine leadership and management tasks simultaneously. For example, when walking the grounds of the school to inspect the facility, one also can greet people and chat, thus building rapport, trust, and relationships while taking care of a management responsibility.

The Bureaucratic and Operational Tasks: Policies, Procedures, Manuals, and Forms (Will I Be Leaving the Job Before I Am Familiar With Each Form?)

Principals have to learn how to maintain records required by federal, state, and local laws including (but not limited to) finances, the instructional program, health, fire, food service, crisis procedures, and attendance. Besides maintaining records, principals need to understand state and district policies and must manage these policies, procedures, and regulations at the school level. Learning how to prepare reports for the district and state takes time because one usually needs to learn how to follow a state or local bureaucratic format. In addition, in very small school districts, principals might be responsible for supervising the school transportation systems as well.

It seems that each school has a myriad of forms. Learning which forms are really important and which ones are not will take the newcomer time. Often secretaries can help with this learning process; some have made principals' books of different forms along with explanations and completed examples to provide helpful guidelines. Keeping a paper trail, with the help of the classified and certified staff, will become important. (Computer technology has enabled us to reduce the paper trail to some extent, but the possibility of a system crashing before files are backed up always is a risk; making hard copies of important documents is critical.) One principal commented, "Just when I figured out the purpose of each form, it was time to leave for the next job."

The district office, as well as state and federal governments, require specific forms and a record of expenses, activities, and enrollment figures. These forms are for purchase orders, preliminary budgetary estimates, field trips, textbook requisitions, instructional technology purchases and servicing, professional development, and average daily attendance (ADA), to name just a few. Having been "bureaucratically challenged" during one's previous "teacher life" is not a satisfactory excuse for failing to follow federal, state, and district expectations. Failure to meet a deadline could cost a school money and human resources and could affect student opportunities to learn.

In addition to the forms, each new principal must learn the federal and state codes, district policies, and school site rules and regulations. State codes for principals can range from a thin manual in one state to a tome almost 1,000 pages long in another state. Figuring out the school and district software for attendance, discipline, student records, and budgetary allocations will take a while, and the software operating system itself might not be one with which you are familiar. Although computer technology and constantly upgraded software generally has increased efficiency, it has added another "need to know" area for principals. There is no way around these challenges; one just has to be ready for them. They will likely not make or break one's principalship, but one does need to figure out the forms and systems that keep the operation going. Although these responsibilities sometimes are referred to as "administrivia" or the housekeeping chores, they need to be completed. An important long-term objective should be to reduce district and school red tape to make life easier for everyone.

Budget and Finances (Will I Ever Understand the Budgetary Process?)

A budget is a financial plan. Most principals are responsible for preparing and administering the school budget within their own buildings. A detailed school budget serves as a blueprint of the major programs of a school and critical areas of concern. An experienced budgetary eye can examine a school budget and recognize important programs and the particular curriculum or staff development direction that a school is pursuing. Actual decision-making authority regarding the role of the principal in the budgetary process varies a great deal from school to school, from district to district, and from state to state. Much depends on how active the district is in the process. Roles and responsibilities vary from the school site to the district depending on state and district policies as well as on individual superintendents, district business managers, school boards, department chairpersons and coordinators, and (more recently) site-based councils.

A concern for all principals is understanding the budgeting and specific accounting procedures in their schools. Concerns arise over issues such as the budgetary categories (e.g., textbooks), the coding of items (e.g., "100" for social studies texts), budgetary time lines, whether funds can be used for one program or another, who should be involved in the process, what happens when there is a shortfall, possibilities for transferring funds from one line to another, maximizing allocations based on student attendance, and student activity funds. For example, figuring out whether an instructional item is a textbook or workbook, or a consumable or nonconsumable, can have far-reaching implications for budgeting. Or, should the new laser disc player be purchased from the library budget or the science budget?

(Experienced principals might continue to have difficulties with budgetary categories; however, they usually come up with a system. It might not make any rational sense to anyone other than the individual principal, but it works for him or her.)

The size of the school district will determine, to a great extent, the type of budgetary challenges one encounters. The larger districts have categories spelled out carefully and have several employees in the district offices working on fiscal issues. But a problem with large bureaucracies is that it might be difficult to find someone on whom you can depend when questions arise. In smaller districts, principals often work alone on budgets and can talk directly with superintendents about monetary issues. In the smallest districts, principals might have to justify each budgetary item with the school board. This might be the case, for example, in a combined principal-superintendent position.

Principals also are concerned with the ADA or full-time equivalency (FTE) enrollment figures because those figures determine a major portion of the funds and staff to which their schools are entitled from state revenues. For example, in the state of Washington, the FTE determines how many teachers, classified staff members, and administrators a school can hire. During the 1995-1996 school year, kindergarten through Grade 3 schools had 54.3 teachers per 1,000 students, whereas Grades 4 through 12 schools had 46 teachers per 1,000 students. The FTE also determines the amount of instructional material allocated for each student. A principal must quickly learn how to calculate these figures accurately to make sure that the school receives the maximum funding possible. It is more complicated than just adding up daily attendance; for example, schools can receive credit for part-time students and special education students. Missing these possibilities can cost schools funding.

Site-Based Decision Making and the Budget

Many schools across the nation are experimenting with site-based decision making. A key tenet of the site-based philosophy is that allocation of school funds at the school site should be decided by the site council. However, the extent of a site council's involvement in budgetary issues will vary. Each site-based team will be different depending on state laws, district policies, and the school culture and needs. As noted in Chapter 5, many principals are newcomers to

site-based decision making. Although a principal might have partici-
pated as a members of a team while a teacher, the principal's role
affords a different perspective.

A principal not yet familiar with the budgetary process is in a
difficult position if he or she is expected to give advice to the council
about how to allocate funds. There might be general guidelines based
on a school's mission statement and last year's budget. However,
newcomers still are learning how to budget field trips (e.g., how field
trip transportation expenses can be reduced) and whether the plea
for new resources from the science department is a yearly demand or
a response to statewide expected curriculum changes or new standards.

Activity and Student Body Funding: A Challenge for Middle and High Schools

Almost every textbook on budgetary issues includes a section on
student body activity funding (Burrup, 1977; Gorton, 1980; Kaiser,
1995). This is a challenging issue for most principals because it can
be one of the most mismanaged budgetary areas. There are many
reasons for mismanagement, but a major cause is simply that one
might have a problem whenever money changes hands. Student
body officers often are required to sign student activity bills beginning in middle school. A teacher serving as a student body adviser
understandably is more concerned with his or her teaching than with
the accuracy of the student body budget. The principal frequently is
left with the responsibility of accurately accounting for student body
funds.

Unions, Associations, the Master Contract, and Grievances

All principals worry that when a grievance is filed against them, it is
an indication of failure. One usually ponders, "What could I have
done to avoid the grievance?" Frizzel (1995) reminds us that when
zero grievances are filed against a principal, one should not neces-
sarily interpret that statistic as positive. It might be that the principal
is "backing off" on every issue. It is natural to want to avoid creating
waves. Experienced principals know that a small contractual issue
can develop into a major battle.

Fearing grievances, some principals maintain that unions or teacher associations inhibit one's ability to treat teachers as colleagues:

Principals' voices:

We're very restricted about what we can and cannot do. So, it [the contract] takes away our humanity in dealing with people. And that humanism then comes back to us and says, "You don't care about me as a teacher," when that isn't it at all. I have to live by the contract because if I don't, then I'm going to be on the carpet for it.

Some people are just here to put in their time, and if it's not in their contract, they don't want to do it. When I first started teaching, there was a job to be done, and we got the job done. . . . But, I think a lot of professionalism has been lost because of all this collective bargaining and master contract.

On the other hand:

As far as the master contract, that's an excellent format; it provides a basis from which I can work. . . . If something is wrong and I can go to the master contract, it makes it easier for me to show the line relationships and how it's set out. So, the collective bargaining for me is not a problem at all.

A Different Union Look:
Is the Change Here to Stay?

An interesting development that principals have to carefully observe and respond to is the apparent changing nature of unions. This development might be a positive challenge for school leaders. Previously, unions were most concerned with due process issues regarding grievances, job security, better salaries, and working conditions. Today, with teachers having a stronger voice, union spokespersons maintain that they are more concerned with improving the quality of teaching and concentrating on staff development.

The changes have led to new and challenging issues. For example, opinions differ regarding how to handle issues such as rewarding excellent teachers, implementing teacher-supported waiver provisions to drop certain contract agreements, and using mentor teachers to assist colleagues (Checkley, 1996). Waivers, for instance, could change the duration and frequency of faculty meetings and increase the number of classes, student enrollment, duration of classes, and staff development options.

Using mentor teachers can be an especially sensitive issue. Although most mentoring literature suggests that mentoring should be distinctly separate from evaluation, school districts are looking for helpful ways in which to assist at-risk teachers. Yet, if the mentoring of a teacher colleague who is at risk is unsuccessful, then will the comments of the mentor become part of the principal's documentation to dismiss the teacher? This would place the union (and the mentor teacher) in a very difficult position, one that is unprecedented. For all principals, the "new union" thinking might be very complicated. Most observers of the educational scene believe that unions will continue on this path because public schools are feeling the pressure of voucher programs, charter schools, and the continued public and political outcry to improve the quality of our schools.

The Legal Quagmire

Principals often comment that school law is one of the most important classes in their school administration programs. With *Brown v. Board of Education* and *Tinker v. Des Moines,* the courts began to take an active role in schools. The courts have indicated that schools cannot avoid the issues of society and must provide, within reason, the same freedoms that exist outside of the schools. Moreover, our society has become much more litigious. If a child breaks his or her arm in the school playground, then a school might face a lawsuit. If a parent is not pleased with a child's class placement, then a variety of legal issues could emerge relating to sex discrimination, racism, tracking, handicapped placement, or disciplinary intervention.

Today, principals have to be familiar with due process laws, implications of student disciplinary decisions, suspension and expulsion procedures, federal and state laws for special education and education of the handicapped, teacher dismissal laws and time lines, safety procedures and liability, search and seizure laws, free speech parameters, and gender equity laws. All principals understandably are concerned with making sure that they handle suspensions properly and that Individualized Educational Programs are correctly administered for special education students. Chapter 11 will provide important guidelines for coping with the legal quagmire.

The School Facility: Is It Safe, Secure, and Used Effectively?

Keeping a school building safe has two dimensions. First, are the students secure and safe—from one another and from dangerous adults living in the community? This is a disciplinary and security issue. Second, are the school building, grounds, and equipment safe for student use? This is a school facility, safety, and management issue. Part of the principalship acculturation process is learning about a school's physical environment. Gaining familiarity with the new environment and learning about facility safety are utmost concerns. In a large middle or high school, this learning process will take a while. In addition to safety concerns, the newcomer needs to consider whether the facility is being used to maximally address the needs of the students and skills of the faculty.

The most difficult areas to which principals must initially orient themselves might be the physical education facilities (e.g., gymnasiums, outdoor fields, locker rooms, weight training rooms), libraries, technology centers, cafeterias, theaters, and band/orchestra classrooms. These facilities often are vast, a distance from the principal's office, and structured differently in almost every school. Spending time circulating throughout their new buildings until they are comfortable with and oriented to each area will enable principals to identify safety hazards and allow facilities usage data to emerge.

Community Use of School Facilities

Community use of a school facility is a major concern. A principal has to get a feel for the community's role in the school before making any major decisions or changes. A new principal does not know how much a facility should be used by outside organizations, and new possibilities arise each year, especially as schools are picking up responsibilities that previously were handled by parents. A school can be positively rewarded when levy time comes if the school site is a productive facility for the general adult community including active senior citizen voters. Yet, principals should exercise caution regarding community facility use because it can be painful to see a facility deteriorate because of after-school and evening use, often with inadequate supervision. Finally, a principal new to a site might not get a true picture of the community's involvement in the school until working a full year on the job because the school year is a cycle of school and community activities.

The Holy Grail: How Does the Informal Network Operate?

Learning the informal procedures of a school can help principals cut through the daily red tape of a school district bureaucracy. For example, newcomers have expressed concern with how to circumvent the bureaucratic system if a deadline passes and a school needs immediate delivery of a textbook series (Garberina, 1980). Until a principal knows who can really get things done in the school and district office, the newcomer will be saddled with using the conventional system. Questions raised by a principal about the system might include the following. What is the best time to call the assistant superintendent (or, in smaller districts, the superintendent)? Who will not mind being contacted during the weekend about an issue (e.g., secretaries, teachers, administrators, custodian)? Who do I need to talk with to find out how the superintendent will feel about an issue? Which teachers have clout at the district office concerning teaching and learning? Which veteran principal in the district can help me organize the budget? How much can I really spend from school funds to help students without having to go through a formal approval process? Additional questions extend to finding helpful community businesses, knowing which substitute teachers can be relied on, and how to get quick approval for a special lighting system for the senior prom.

Principals need to learn which district policies and procedures are "sacred," which need to be "sort of" followed, and which can be ignored. Finding out which veteran principal in the district to ask such questions can be risky. Asking the "wrong" veteran—the one who always follows procedures—may lead some to believe that the principal new to the district is manipulating the system (which might be true).

PART TWO

Finding Solutions to the Challenges and Problems: Strategies, Advice, and Insights for Success

The chapters in this part examine ways of coping with the challenges and problems that principals face. The socialization process for a brand new principal, or a seasoned principal hired at another site, will simply take time as one learns about the community, learns about the new facility, learns to cope with the loneliness and time frustrations, and learns about key certificated and classified personnel. As the socialization progresses, the principal begins to understand the unique school culture of which he or she is now a part and also develops a sense of security and comfort with work. A vision of what is right for the school community will start to crystallize. Allies in the school and district will emerge. The uncharted waters will appear a bit less treacherous.

CHAPTER 7

Becoming a Lifelong Learner

Developing the habits of being a *lifelong learner* in the principalship is an important theme of this book. The significance of becoming successfully acculturated through a desire to observe and learn each day cannot be overemphasized. Ideally, any individual taking on the principal's role should begin the job by embracing characteristics of the lifelong learner. This chapter provides suggestions to help one appreciate and cultivate this critical characteristic.

Embracing the Socialization Process

Going through a period in which one trips over hurdles that everyone else appears to avoid can be very frustrating. Yet, that is the fate of all individuals who take on new jobs. However, as noted in Chapter 1, instead of perceiving this period with fear, one should view this period as a special time of learning. A newcomer's antennas always are picking up information that he or she might miss when life becomes routine. Embrace this period as a welcome and unique opportunity to become part of a new organization that you are shaping and by which you are being shaped.

As you become a part of a new organization, notice that your loyalties will begin to shift from your present school to the school of your new principalship. By reflecting on this natural phenomenon, you will have a better understanding of your feelings and the transition and why things look so much better where you are going. Recall that shifting your loyalties is known as "leave taking," a very normal process (Louis, 1980). By way of illustration, a school principal aware of leave taking always cautioned teachers who accepted jobs in other schools of the possibility of starting to "bad mouth" the present school with colleagues. It is easy for teachers leaving a school to let colleagues know how fortunate they were to be leaving an "inadequate" organization. This principal would ask departing staff members to make a special effort to be positive about the school during their last few months. Furthermore, the principal asked these professionals to share suggestions to improve the school by letting her know what works well and what should be changed. Immediately following their new appointments, principals "to be" and veteran principals should work harder than ever to leave their present organizations on a positive note.

The immediate period following one's selection into a new organization (i.e., the anticipatory socialization stage) is a perfect time in which to learn about the organizational culture of the new school by finding out about its history and the community it serves. Ideally (if you are not hired a week or so before the school year begins), the newly appointed principal should set up regular meetings with the leader being replaced. Working to ensure a smooth transition with the departing principal can help set a positive tone for the next year. This can be critical for the newcomer who replaces a "principal icon." Seeing the two leaders together can be a powerful image for the staff. Sitting in the back of the auditorium during graduation, attending a spring sports event, carefully reviewing the yearbook, and paying attention to rituals (e.g., how retiring staff are honored) can give one invaluable insights into the organization. Of course, the newly hired principal should be sensitive to the departing colleague and the specific circumstances. But the newcomer should take advantage of opportunities offered by the departing veteran. Of particular import is learning about how staff members perceive the newcomer in relation to the current situation. For example, did any of them apply for the principalship?

Recognizing in advance that you will feel unprepared for the job is an important first step that can be of some relief to the newcomer. Yes, you will feel lonely. But knowing that the loneliness is normal and that it is okay to have this feeling as part of the socialization process is significant. The loneliness does not have to become a permanent state for the newcomer who takes initiative and networks with other principals and teaching colleagues. Pick up that phone and discuss your problems with another principal or a trusted colleague. In addition, e-mailing colleagues can reduce the isolation; a humorous message can help one get through the day.

The encounter stage of the socialization process usually is less of a shock for the newcomer who can reflect on the process. Reflecting, however, might not make the job easier. But by reflecting, one will know that the feelings and anxieties experienced are a normal part of the journey regardless of how many years one has spent in the principalship. Thus, it helps to understand challenges of the encounter stage such as the complexity of adult relationships, perceived distance from the students, the importance of broadening one's view, and the difficulty of remaining focused on the instructional vision. Developing effective habits during the encounter stage can help the newcomer keep his or her eyes on a strategic vision of teaching and learning while simultaneously getting the daily work done.

Awareness of the socialization process also helps the newcomer keep a perspective and can help one reflect on "progress" from the experience of the encounter stage to that of the insider stage, when one is accepted into the organization. Understanding the importance of moving toward the insider stage should help the principal work to develop trust with the faculty, to be visible for the students, to become familiar with the facility, and to actively listen to parents and the broader community. To be an insider, one has to network actively with peers and colleagues as well. Understanding this should motivate the newcomer to attend social events as well as regional, state, and national conferences.

The transitional period will be different for each principal. However, understanding that you are going through a process is important. Taking on a principalship is not simply closing one door and opening another. For many, it can be the most significant learning experience of one's lifetime.

Principals: Always Asking Questions

A principal's voice:

Go in and honestly say "I don't know everything there is to know. . . . I'll probably be meeting myself coming this year, and any help you can give me I'd really appreciate. And be honest with me if I'm doing something wrong."

Bennis and Nanus (1985) stress that leading chief executive officers are great askers of questions. Leaders want to know about their organizations and are not shy or intimidated about asking when they do not know the answers. Any newcomer needs to ask a lot of questions. Do not worry about fulfilling a personal "I am all-knowing" myth. You are not all-knowing, and you know it; the sooner the faculty realizes that you are not going to act out this myth, the sooner you will have the opportunity to build some trust. Asking questions is essential for any principal who wants to know about policies, procedures, regulations, or a myriad of other things. Ask the teachers about the curriculum, ask the computer coordinator about the new software system, ask the secretary about how folks are greeted over the phone, and call the district business manager about the budget codes and the difference between consumables and nonconsumables. This does not mean that the people being asked the questions are running the show; it just means that you are seeking to understand policies, procedures, and practices to better serve students. This is especially so for the principal hired outside of the district who has less of an understanding of the school culture. One principal seeking to understand operating procedures offered to substitute for individuals working within the organization to better understand the organization from inside out.

This willingness to ask questions and learn about the organization is not only a survival technique but also a technique that should develop into a habit as you become more experienced in the job. This habit increases your chances for success as a leader. An effective principal asks a lot of questions 10 years into the job. In addition, the "learning leader" attends workshops, shares information and articles with the staff, remains for the whole session when a faculty workshop is conducted, listens to faculty and parents, and shows a willingness to listen to students as they present their work.

The act of asking questions sets a tone in the school that, in effect, states, "It is okay to ask questions. Each day, we are learning from one another." Collectively, this act, along with others, develops a culture of an ethically aligned learning community because administrators, teachers, parents, and students all are expected to ask questions.

Embracing Principles of the Change Process

The learning leader seeks to understand principles of the change process to interpret daily interactions and reactions, to plan, and sometimes to console. How individuals respond to change can differ dramatically depending on how vested they are in the change, what else is going on in their lives, at what adult stages of life they are, and who is promoting the change. Facilitating change involves considering a variety of factors, some of which include pondering the following. What is the financial, philosophical, and emotional cost of the change? How complex will the change be to implement? What else is this change effort competing with? How many cohorts of individuals (e.g., parents, teachers, substitutes, paraprofessionals, students) will be affected by the change?

When promoting change, it is useful to consider that organizational change takes place one individual at a time. Facilitating change involves helping organizational members see its relevance, involving individuals to develop ownership, demonstrating how it is feasible to make the change a reality, and building and maintaining trust and rapport in the process. Expect that major change efforts usually will take 3 to 5 years to accomplish, and heed the words of one principal who commented as she shrugged, "Sometimes you gotta go slow to go fast."

Networking

A principal's voice:

Go to . . . your peers and the person who was in the job before you. Don't be afraid to get up and say, "Gee, what did you do in this instance?" I didn't do that. I have [done so] lately when I can't find something in the files or whatever.

Lifelong learners can gain inspiration and insight from colleagues. The antidote for that loneliness is networking. Network with individuals, network in small and large groups, and attend conferences. One to one, find out who the helpful mentors are in your district and call them, e-mail them, visit their schools, take them out for coffee, invite them to your house for dinner, and/or attend their workshops during state and national conferences. Seek out retired principals and ask them to visit your school. Engage in shadowing other principals to gain various perspectives on getting the job done.

It is imperative to attend professional meetings. One might think, "I can't miss school for these 2 days," but one's professional development is critical. Teachers and students need to see you as a learner, just as they are learners in an ethically aligned organization. Principals can, in turn, share their learning at school through presentations, offering their notes, informal book or article reviews, videotapes, or audiotapes. Learning in this way flows through the organization. Professional meetings are great opportunities for recharging one's professional batteries, networking, and reflecting on one's performance. What are other principals doing? What are the issues among other rookie or veteran principals who have accepted new positions?

Principals' voices:

I think a seminar kind of thing [would be helpful]. . . . For instance, there are several new administrators . . . [and] we have talked about meeting after work, having a glass of wine and talking, sharing. But between their schedules and mine, it's just not happening. . . . [A] university could pull that together for us. It's like teachers, if you get together with teachers [and] share, you improve your instructional management strategy. Administrators need to do that too. I'd like to know how other people handle that god-awful lunchroom. Do they walk around with the big voice . . . and demand? Are there some secrets to managing that where it's still comfortable and yet not appalling?

On the other hand:

My experience has been that there is plenty of that [administrative contact] because of all the meetings you go to together [laugh]. You know, so there's a lot of that. I feel comfortable picking up the phone and interacting with them that way. Now today, the principal from one of the other schools is coming over to see me, so I can show him how I am setting up my classes. . . . So, we share ideas.

Broadening One's View

A principal's voice:

Step back, look at the whole picture, and then step in again.

Perspective taking is a powerful leverage point for the instructional leader. It allows one to see a situation in a different light. It might be necessary for the instructional leader to reflect privately on one's beliefs to find out where he or she stands regarding a school's needs. A journal is a perfect vehicle for this reflective exercise. One's written comments might indicate a bias favoring a subject that one has taught. It is easy to develop a skeptical position on a topic with which one is unfamiliar or, more revealing, a subject area in which one was unsuccessful as a student. Broadening one's views means becoming flexible and open to the best of each school. Possibly one of the most significant aspects of Gardner's (1985) work on the seven "intelligences" is that it raised our consciousness about each type of intelligence. Goleman's (1995) work on emotional intelligence, which suggests that about 80% of adult success is based on emotional intelligence (the ability to get along with others and work out crises), implies that schools need to offer more than success in a particular subject area to help students through life. It is satisfying to have the best marching band in the state or the best advanced placement calculus scores, but it is not enough.

Broadening one's view and "walking the talk" about honoring each school program can profoundly affect the school's ecosystem. The ecosystem concept—balancing the needs of the different parts of the school and recognizing that we depend on one another for success—helps the principal understand the importance of broadening one's views. The message from the leader is, "We bring strength to one another by bringing strength to each program." Understanding the ecosystem of a school reminds a principal to encourage each teacher to dismiss students on time after a period so that they can arrive on time for the next class. The math teacher might think it is okay to keep students a few minutes longer (e.g., "My class is more important"), but the students might then be late for the English class. By encouraging teachers to honor the time commitment, a principal is reminding everyone of the importance of each subject and our dependence on one another. The English as a Second Language (ESL) teacher should walk into the principal's office and know that he or she is just as important as the football coach whose team won the state championship yesterday. This is the challenge that faces all principals. To emphasize shared support within the school as an ecosystem, consider having the football coach introduce the ESL assembly program and have the ESL department chair introduce the football coach at the pep rally. Symbolic gestures such as these communicate powerful messages.

Another aspect of broadening one's view is recognizing how various life experiences all can be preparation for the principalship. For example, performing in high school or college drama productions certainly can help a principal with public speaking, working on group projects, and meeting deadlines. When in the principalship, one needs to be a risk taker about activities to prepare for the myriad of events that will occur. When attending workshops, consider going to sessions that have little to do with your subject area of expertise to gain an understanding of each school department. A perfect opportunity for a high school principal, formerly a history teacher, might be a conference on Shakespeare. Attending a "Math Their Way" summer workshop might be a prudent choice for an elementary principal who never felt comfortable with math manipulates. Each experience will come in handy at one time or another.

A principal's voice:

I think a broad training is necessary. The attendant things that one deals with in a day, it's unbelievable. I've had everything from a hamster's eye falling out, to frozen pipes, to dealing with regular things about kids and teachers. I think a person needs to be flexible.

Developing Effective Problem-Solving Habits

Habits are behaviors that we carry out routinely. Lifelong learners need to develop effective problem-solving habits that become part of a repertoire that enables them to make sound decisions. Principals make hundreds of decisions each day, just as teachers do. The difficult part is making good decisions as a result of practical problem-solving skills. In the principalship, most problems have to be solved relatively quickly—sometimes almost instantly. It is a luxury to have the time for reflective problem solving. It would be very difficult to convince experienced principals that any problem-solving model has much practical use unless the model helps them make on-the-spot quality decisions. Each principal needs to put into practice skills that will become routine, or become habits, for both quick decisions and those made under less time pressure. These lifelong problem-solving habits include the following.

1. *A proactive approach toward problems.* Principals need to keep their eyes open about potential difficulties before they emerge as major problems. To hope that the difficulties will go away only results in more problems. School discipline is a case in point. An Alberta junior high school proactively changed its approach to discipline because of perceived and actual behavioral changes in the student body (Litke, 1996). The school decided to respond to the challenge before it became overwhelming. Litke (1996) recommends the following for schools:

> Be proactive in dealing with student violence. If violence is not a problem at your school, do not assume that it cannot become a problem. Make safety part of your mission and values. Have a clear policy in place, and notify all stakeholders about it. (p. 79)

Although the junior high school used a top-down approach to develop the disciplinary policy, the faculty and parents supported the initiative because it was proactive and thoughtful and addressed potentially serious disciplinary incidents that could negatively affect the school's mission.

2. *Identifying the problem and considering the source.* Identifying the important elements of a problem situation and gaining information on possible causes is a critical step in problem solving (Thomson, 1993). Gorton and Snowden (1993) emphasize that identifying the source of information concerning a problem can be a helpful problem-solving clue. For example, the administration needs to consider the source if a local parent, who has been having difficulty with a few students smoking near her house during lunchtime, notifies the school that 90% of the student body smokes. The immediate problem is not the number of students smoking; it is to stop students from smoking in front of the parent's house. After resolving the immediate problem, the school needs to address the open campus issue and, most important, proactive and preventive health measures to reduce student smoking.

When faced with the luxury of a couple of days in which to make a decision, one principal checked with his mentor. The mentor, an experienced elementary principal, once remarked that "part of being a school leader is knowing when to break the rules." When time was unavailable to talk with the mentor, the new principal would take a moment and think, "Now, what would [the mentor] identify as the problem and do in this situation?" As a principal gets to know the faculty, he or she will gain confidence concerning which teachers should be consulted about difficulties and who can be trusted to provide helpful information to assist students.

3. *Considering the significant negative consequences and deadlines when problem solving.* Gorton and Snowden (1993) address the important commonsense notion of prioritizing problems and judging the importance of each problem by considering the possible negative consequences if the problem is mishandled or ignored. This is a practical suggestion that should become part of one's problem-solving repertoire. It also is suggested that one should consider the deadline for resolving a problem as part of the prioritizing process. For example, a major problem for a school might be inadequate wiring for new technology hardware that will be arriving in late May. However, with the summer vacation months approaching, the deadline for completing the wiring can move from May to August. This will "bump" the wiring issue down the priority list. On the other hand, a defective traffic light only a half block from a school needs to be fixed at once because of possible tragic and immediate consequences.

4. *Examining alternative solutions and implementing the decision.* After identifying a problem, gaining practical information on it, considering the source, considering negative consequences if mishandled, and considering the time line for decision making, a principal should have enough information to make a decision. One should try to develop alternative solutions and consider the consequences of each choice. When the final decision is made, one hopes it will be the best choice. Certainly, minimizing negative consequences should weigh as an essential reason for the selected solution as a result of the decision-making process.

5. *Reflecting on the problem-solving process.* When quick decisions are made, there is no time for reflection on the process. However, the

day-to-day reality of the principalship should not stand as a long-term hurdle to improving our efficiency in reflective decision making. It is valuable to reflect when time permits. This can be in the evening while writing in one's journal or sharing thoughts with a spouse, at a conference while discussing problems and solutions with colleagues, or with an administrator or a teacher at the school. Through reflection, one learns, adds strategies to one's repertoire, and (in this way) enhances the quality of future decisions. As a consequence, all members of the school community benefit.

To summarize, effective problem solving needs to become a habit for school principals so that, whenever possible, they can operate other than by the "seat of their pants." Key problem-solving strategies include a proactive approach, problem identification, gaining information on problem causes, judging the source of information, identifying possible negative consequences resulting from the problem, setting deadlines for problem resolution, considering alternative solutions, implementing the solution, and reflecting on the problem-solving process.

CHAPTER 8

Human Relations and Authentic Communication

Listening well is often silent but never passive.

Nichols (1995, p. 113)

Active Listening

When administrative interns and their mentor principals were asked at the end of their internships, "What are the critical skills for a principalship," an oft-repeated answer was *active listening*. A mentor principal commented that by listening, one can "convince people that you care about them. It's people and relationships. . . . Organizational and systems stuff comes after that" (Alvy, 1997, p. 11). The connection between positive human relations and communicating effectively was a firm theme from both the experienced professionals and the interns.

The importance of communication is found throughout the administrative literature. The emphasis on active listening skills is especially critical if schools are going to be democratic organizations with widespread decision-making possibilities. Interestingly, the National Policy Board for Educational Administration (NPBEA) identified *sensitivity* as one of its 21 domains, or standards, of leadership. The importance of active listening within the sensitivity domain is apparent with expectations such as "perceiving the needs and concerns of others . . . working with others in emotionally stressful situations or in conflict . . . obtaining feedback . . . [and] recognizing multicultural sensibilities" (Thomson, 1993, Section 15, pp. 1-23).

The principal should be the number one advocate and model for healthy communication in a school. The leader who is a successful communicator takes a giant step toward success. Too frequently, we think of communication as "our talking" or waiting for "our turn to talk." Sadly, we often do not listen to what others are saying and sometimes are convinced that what we have to say is more important. Communication expert Michael Nichols stressed, "The urge to be recognized is so compelling that even when we do listen, it's usually not with the intent to understand, but to reply" (Nichols, 1995, p. 246). This can be a serious flaw in a principal when attempting to build faculty trust. Trust is built up slowly, and the time a principal takes to listen to colleagues is a building block for a trusting relationship. It is unfortunate if one fails to take advantage of the ideas and expertise of a group by failing to listen.

One principal who knew he had to improve his listening skills placed a small yellow dot on the wall above the office couch where most people sat when speaking with him. He placed the yellow dot as a personal reminder to listen to the valuable thoughts of others. He could always see the dot above the couch, and the reminder came in handy as he developed his listening skills. After a meeting, he would ask himself, "Was I an effective listener?"

One often forgets a name when introduced to a new colleague largely because there is a thought happening at the same time a name is mentioned: What shall I say next? A strategy for remembering names—a critical skill for any effective communicator—is to *decide to remember*. Focus on the name. Listen. Repeat the name in a sentence: "So, Bob, where did you work previously?" Rehearse it in your mind. The ability is valuable because people feel their names are important.

Assessing and Using Our Various Communication Skills

In addition to listening skills, principals need to consider their other communication strengths and weaknesses. The NPBEA lists both oral expression and written expression (Thomson, 1993) as critical domains and recommends that each leader assess his or her skills in these areas. Do you write clear and concise memos, or are you better at longer reports? How do you feel about speaking with small groups? With large groups? One on one?

A variety of communication strategies are necessary to succeed in the principalship. Work on the other communication skills when you can. Principals need to use different skills as they interact with the faculty, students, and community. Methods of communication might include memos, small group meetings, brief one-on-one chats (probably the most frequent form of communication), extended one-on-one meetings, large assemblies, e-mail, phone calls, daily bulletins, video announcements, morning public address announcements, and posted master calendars of key school events.

Providing essential information for faculty, parents, and students is proactive problem solving. For example, posting a large copy of the district master calendar of events in a middle or high school faculty lounge and providing individual copies for faculty members will help teachers plan exams and major projects. Moreover, the master calendar will reduce the possibility and pressure of having to schedule an event that was not initially programmed for the year.

Recently, as schools have become more technologically advanced, daily video broadcasts, text on videos, and e-mail are being used in classrooms to communicate daily announcements to students and faculty. However, as with public address announcements, use of video announcements should be limited to minimize classroom interruptions. Principals send the message to teachers that classroom time is vital by limiting administrative and student use of the schoolwide public address system. Except for emergencies, announcements should be limited to homeroom periods. Furthermore, if students in only five classrooms need to be contacted about an event, then why announce the event to the whole school? It might take principals and secretaries longer to contact the five rooms by telephone or memo, but it will maximize learning time. Just 5 minutes saved daily adds up to about 15 hours of instructional time in a year.

In general, e-mail is an excellent vehicle for communication, although it should not be considered a substitute for important interpersonal interactions. This is true of technology in general. Technology is a powerful tool in the hands of school administrators, secretaries, teachers, and students. However, it is unwise to assume that a decorated memo or creatively displayed idea is a more effective means of communication than is human interaction and dialogue. There is no substitute for a smile, patient listening, or interpreting one's body language. Some communication experts suggest that 70% of all communication occurs nonverbally. A teacher might say over the phone, "Sure, I'll be glad to chaperone the game Saturday night." Yet, it would help to be able to read body language to know whether the teacher really wants to chaperone.

Communicating With Various On-Site School Groups That Often Are Overlooked: Specialist Teachers, Students, Classified Staff, Teacher Assistants, and Student Teachers

Each professional colleague in a school should feel that the principal treats him or her with respect and honors his or her role. A principal sends a strong message to the classified staff if the staff members see that they will receive the same respect as teachers. As the most visible school official, the principal must realize that his or her behaviors are noticed by others—especially students. How does the principal speak with regular classroom teachers? With specialist teachers? The custodian? Teacher assistants? Food service personnel? Security personnel? Bus drivers? Students? Ethical alignment again becomes an important theme. One should practice ethical and respectful behavior with everyone.

Specialist Teachers

Specialists value feeling that they are as important as regular classroom teachers—and, of course, they are. How a principal organizes an elementary faculty meeting can send a strong message to specialists. Are the meeting activities only for regular classroom teachers? If a reading program is being evaluated during a meeting, then the principal, or the team organizing the meeting, needs to include the physical education specialists in the group discussions or excuse the specialists from attending. It would be best to include the specialists and find important discussion roles for them. As interdisciplinary and thematic teaching is gaining prominence in most schools, it often is fruitful to actively involve art, phyical education, music, English as a second language, technology, and other specialists during faculty meetings. Their perspectives should be valued.

Classified Staff and Students

Classified staff members, especially school secretaries, are in very sensitive positions. They can make or break a school's public relations image by how they answer the phone or receive school visitors. In addition, in middle and high schools, students often assist in the office with answering phones and receiving visitors. Classified staff members and students will carefully watch how the principal handles visitors and take cues from the principal's behavior.

It is a good idea to let the office and food service staff members know how you feel about respecting each member of the community by sharing information with them at meetings and modeling respect for them. Probably the most prudent approach during a meeting would be to simply state, "I know that you are already showing respect for each member of the school community, and I just want you to know that I will continue that policy." Certainly, suggestions and ideas from everyone invited to the meeting will be important. Providing examples of what you will expect with short role-plays and examples of greetings might be helpful. Still, the staff will not be convinced that you respect each individual until you show it through your behavior, that is, until you "walk the talk." Demonstrating respect communicates what is valued and also celebrates desired practices. Respect for classified staff members also is important because some of these individuals might play vital cultural roles.

Teacher Assistants and Student Teachers

Teacher assistants, teaching aides, and student teachers also are in sensitive positions. Teacher assistants usually have close ties to the community and have children in the school. Assistants sometimes have teaching certificates and simply are unable to secure jobs. They might be working toward certification. Regardless of their degree status or positions in a school, students, administration, and faculty must display respect for teaching assistants. This is not a problem with younger children; they usually consider the assistants "regular teachers." Importantly, when individuals feel respected and included, a feeling of common commitment and service is generated in pursuit of a common goal—serving students.

Principals need to let assistants know that their primary duty is to assist teachers to help students reach their potentials. Principals set a strong example for both teachers and students by communicating respectfully with assistants. In addition, it is important to let students know that disrespectful behavior with teacher assistants is as unacceptable as disrespectful behavior with teachers or the principal.

Student teachers might be the most fragile individuals in a school. They often are young, inexperienced, and needing all the help they can get from their supervising teachers, university supervisors, and principals. Principals should invite student teachers to faculty meetings and embrace the student teachers as members of the staff (e.g., obtain classroom keys for them). Student teachers, although working at maximum capacity, often are the first to volunteer to help with student activities; they can be a refreshing source of help. By interacting with student teachers, principals can gain insight concerning which future teachers would be most suitable for hiring.

Creating a Schoolwide Forum for Communication

One new principal characterized the school principal as the "flow-through person"—the source or catalyst for the flow of information. The principal can help to ensure that barriers to healthy communication are reduced and that the free flow of ideas to improve teaching and learning will be facilitated by the administration.

The principal can help to create a forum for individual and group communication by supporting facilities and activities that encourage communication. A faculty lounge does not have to be a dreary room with broken furniture. Rather, it can be an inviting space that is conducive to dialogue. A principal can make sure that a room is available for a group of teachers who want to meet about curriculum standards or a school social activity. Supplying markers, butcher paper, and other meeting tools to teachers for a meeting is a simple but important gesture of support for their activities.

Faculty meetings should include activities that enhance communication. Many principals work with faculty leaders to plan meetings, work out agendas, and ensure that there will be open dialogue. Activities that encourage conversation should be carefully planned so that teacher dialogue is the centerpiece of the meetings and not "administrivia" that can be communicated via conventional memo or electronic mail. Faculty meetings should be in-service opportunities whenever possible—forums for sharing dialogue about teaching and learning. When this occurs, the collective knowledge base about teaching and learning is enhanced and the organization's capacity to serve students becomes greater. Faculty meetings also provide a wealth of perspectives for enriching a school's problem-solving capacity. Setting a tone that encourages professional dialogue in one forum also sets an example for other forums including one-on-one teacher talk during lunch or other informal settings.

Working With Parents and
the General Community

> But, the essential element in my failure to win school board
> and community support was my inability, right from the start,
> to take into account how different my new school, school
> system, and community were from those I was leaving.
>
> *A principal commenting on why he was not*
> *reappointed (quoted in Jentz, 1982, p. 76)*

Parents want a principal to succeed simply because it is in the best interest of the children. It can be tough for a newly hired principal if the principal being replaced had a wonderful district reputation. Was the departing principal a longtime pillar of strength? If he or she was, then it can be a tough act for anyone to follow, whether a rookie principal or a longtime veteran moving to a new district. It will take a while to build trust in the school and community. Initially, it would be prudent to continue much of the old routines to keep the traditions going. If the former principal left with tension in the community, then it should be easier to build relationships because almost everyone wants to see you succeed immediately (although you will have to work extra hard with the inside candidates who were not selected for the principalship).

Again, treating everyone in the parent community with respect is critical. Offering a cup of coffee to reduce tension before meetings, arriving on time for meetings, greeting parents with a smile, taking a few minutes to show a new family the school, and remembering that new child's name tomorrow can go a long way toward building relationships. Some parents did not have positive experiences with principals during their own schooling. Contacting parents about their children to communicate positive news certainly would be a welcome change from the traditional principalship image.

Conducting a Needs Assessment
of Parent Views

To gain insight regarding parent views of the school, it could be helpful to conduct a needs assessment in several areas. This step can be an important proactive strategy concerning parent thoughts about the school and, hopefully, will provide helpful information to make the school a more effective learning community. The needs assessment could seek views on academic success, homework, extracurricular activities, social issues, and transportation. One such needs assessment instrument used in the schools in Charlotte-Mecklenburg, North Carolina, asks parents about school discipline, climate, communication, parent involvement, instruction, and the quality of the administration (Murphy & Pimentel, 1996). The assessment instrument asks questions such as "Is the principal of your school open and available to you?," "Is academic achievement the top priority at this school?," and "Are you satisfied with the principal's leadership?" (p. 78). Another critical source of information is a community newspaper, which may shed light on a community's morale or important community political issues. The information can give a principal insight regarding the culture and climate of the school. Purchasing that newspaper is a must, even if the principal lives outside of the school community.

As a general point, part of working with parents and community is accepting the notion that another area of the principal's responsibility is to seek opinions beyond the schoolhouse, out in the community. A principal should view himself or herself as part of the greater school community. The needs assessment process sends a signal to members of the community that their opinions are important. Organizational theorists would describe this practical idea as an "open-systems" approach to schooling, recognizing that the school is part of the general community rather than closed off from the dynamics of society.

If the school does not have a database on parent and community resource possibilities, then this also could be an area in which to build a link with the parents. For example, finding out which parents would be available for career night or college night and which parents could speak on particular topics can be helpful information for the school and can help strengthen the school community link.

Community Health, Safety, and Social Service Specialists

Today, many students do not receive the support at home that might be necessary, and community support services have become critical. A principal should drive through a neighborhood and notice what agencies are in the immediate school area. Also, one should ask guidance counselors, veteran teachers, and parents about agencies. A call to each agency—including health, child abuse, police, and social support organizations—should be made by the principal introducing himself or herself and expressing appreciation for each organization's services. A visit to each agency or from an agency representative to the school should be an agenda priority. When school and community agencies craft partnerships, services to students are enhanced.

CHAPTER 9

Honoring the
Experienced/Veteran Staff

Know who your staff leaders are. Know the ones that are respected by the balance of the staff. Respect their judgment. Don't be afraid to be wrong. . . . The bottom line is you want things to go smoothly and it doesn't matter if it's your decision or the teacher's. And if they can come up collectively with all the answers, that's fine.

A principal's voice

In the beginning of the school year, new teachers value assistance with logistical and instructional needs to survive. Not only must new teachers learn about classroom responsibilities, but it also is helpful to learn cultural norms, policies, curriculum expectations, and effective teaching strategies. This knowledge can come from experienced teachers or the principal. It is natural for a newly hired principal to gravitate toward and help new teachers, or veteran teachers new to the school, because they will be facing similar difficulties considering that all of them are newcomers. However, for the principal, it probably is just as important to concentrate on establishing a strong professional relationship with the seasoned veterans before strengthening relationships with new teachers. It is the seasoned veterans, with the historical school knowledge, who can provide the principal with important information to succeed during that first year.

Does Any Group Have a
Greater Stake in a Principal's
Success Than the Veteran Staff?

Hart (1993) observes, "By focusing on the principal and under-emphasizing the organization, traditional leadership succession literature fails to adequately address the complex environment in which succession occurs" (p. 130). Part of that complex environment relates to the newcomer's relationship with seasoned teachers. It is easy to state that students always have the greatest stake in the success of a principal. Nevertheless, veteran staff members, working in a school for years, certainly experience anxiety on the arrival of a new principal. Concerns might surface about having to prove themselves again, possibly with a principal 20 years younger than some of the veterans. Issues might include the challenging of personal and professional idiosyncrasies (which had been accepted by the departing principal), teaching philosophies, curriculum expectations, discipline policies, the general direction of the school, and the newcomer's leadership style (e.g., "I was always able to drop in on Peggy [the departing principal]"). The veteran teacher eventually might welcome the change, but until a relationship is established, there will be questions.

Honoring the experienced staff members includes affirming their accomplishments. If change is to be introduced, then principals need to be concerned about the staff member who might think, "I've been doing this for 20 years. . . . Was my approach ineffective? Did I hurt the kids by teaching this way? What am I to do? Maybe I won't be as successful teaching another way." Early on, new principals need to let veterans know that they are going to be thoughtful about discovering how things are done in their schools. Veterans should quickly get the message that the newcomers respect experience.

Strategies to Honor the Veteran Staff
and Affirm a School's Accomplishments

It is important to communicate and create a partnership with veteran staff members as early as possible. A key strategy is to meet with veterans at their convenience before the school year begins. Let them know that you value their accomplishments and long-term dedication to the school. Be mindful of their accomplishments even if the school needs to move in a direction that conflicts with their past performance. Veteran staff members can be powerful in a school, are part of the historical culture, and can be formidable opponents.

By listening to veteran staff members' ideas, principals can gain valuable insight regarding the school culture. For example, why do the veterans do the things they do in the particular ways they do them? The veterans can share important thoughts on school heroes, heroines, traditions, and sacred stories. What is the history of the school's name? Is there a school song? Furthermore, the veteran input can be very helpful when considering changes. Veterans can provide helpful information about an idea that previously failed. They are likely to tell you the advantages and disadvantages of possible changes. Hopefully, the educational rationale for their historical reflections is based on what is best for students. Their historical perspective should help worthwhile ideas find an easier path to success.

Eventually, you will have to challenge veterans who do not act in the best interest of students. Consequently, it is important to take time when developing relationships with the veteran staff to determine who are the student advocates and who might be just biding time (or, as one principal put it, "They retired but forgot to announce it"). When a confrontation must occur, you will be glad that you waited and built trust and alliances for what certainly will be an unpleasant period.

Using Experienced Staff as "Buddies"

A significant way in which to affirm the seasoned staff members is to have them work as mentors with new teachers and at-risk colleagues. First, find out whether a "buddy program" is in place in the school for new teachers. (If a buddy program exists, it can provide a foundation for establishing a mentor program.) A buddy program is an important orientation activity to help new teachers learn about the school instructional and curriculum program as well as the culture of the school and community. Although worth the risk, asking specific veteran staff members to engage in such an activity may be tricky because the principal does not yet know who the most caring, empathetic, and best teachers are for a buddy activity or mentor relationship.

By asking veteran staff members to work with new teachers, the principal is affirming the veterans' status as the recognized school leaders on "how things work around here." Working on the buddy system will give the principal time to build relationships with veteran staff members while sending the following message to new teachers: "I care about you and want to provide camaraderie and professional support to ease your entry into the teaching profession."

The Experienced Assistant Principal

Developing a positive relationship with a veteran assistant principal can be a complicated goal for any new principal. The first issue might relate to whether the assistant principal applied for the principalship. If he or she did apply and was disappointed with the board's decision, then a few rocky months might result. Another issue might relate to the assistant principal's discipline approach and how that approach aligns with the new principal and district policies. A third issue might relate to how close professionally the assistant principal was to the previous principal. They might have developed complementary styles of leadership and well-established routines. Patience and sensitivity will be important factors as new relationships are forged.

The principal should quickly let the assistant principal know that he or she will depend on the assistant principal and establish routine meetings, probably once a week. Until the principal has his or her feet on the ground, it might not be a bad idea to meet daily with the assistant principal either before or after school. The meetings will send an important message to the faculty that the assistant principal will continue to play a major school role.

The early meetings might address school routines, how to avoid major mistakes, and how to keep the ship afloat until the new principal fully understands the operation. The principal should try, early on, to gain insights into how the assistant principal can grow professionally by building on his or her strengths and taking on important responsibilities. Unless an assistant principal wants to remain in that position, the principal should be thinking about how the assistant can broaden his or her skills for a future principalship. The principal must keep in mind that strong leaders delegate responsibilities appropriately and surround themselves with the best available staff.

Veteran Specialists: Teachers and Counselors

Specialist teachers—including English as a Second Language, resource room, and reading specialists as well as computer coordinators— often see themselves as overlooked by principals. As noted in Chapter 8, they wonder, "Does this faculty meeting relate to me?" "Will the principal notice if I'm not at the meeting?" "Does the principal believe in the importance of a guidance program?" The ecosystem concept applies here; each member of the school community contributes to the success of the organization or can help bring the organization down.

Principals can encourage specialist teachers and counselors by asking these professionals to share their expertise with the staff during small group or major faculty meetings. Principals should visit the specialist classrooms and attend staffings so that specialists know that the principals appreciate their contributions to student success.

Veteran Classified Staff

Each school has food service workers, custodians, secretaries, teacher assistants, security personnel, and others who have worked in the school for years and who will be anxious to develop a positive relationship with you. Principalship visibility and one-on-one exchanges with each individual and group are important. Everyone needs to know that you think he or she plays a critical role in the school's success. You should let the custodian know that a clean and safe school gives you personal satisfaction because a school's appearance is a strong indicator of how much individuals care about where they teach and learn. Let the food service workers know that good food carefully prepared and pride in a cafeteria's cleanliness are essential expectations for the good school and are welcomed by its organizational members.

As noted several times, the secretary is critical to many aspects of school success. The principal should be open to secretarial ideas regarding previous managerial strategies. The secretary likely had a very close professional relationship with the former principal, and the adjustment will not be easy. The secretary might "grieve" the loss of the previous principal or be more pleased by the change than any other member of the staff. Where principal and secretary can find common ground is in their continuing commitment to student learning.

Veterans in the District Office

District office personnel can be valuable resources. As a leader of learners, the principal should be open to opportunities to continue to grow professionally. Call key personnel at the district office and introduce yourself. During the initial conversations, ask what they think would be critical knowledge or advice to have and what they value in school leadership. District personnel often are former school principals and can serve as mentors. Developing a good professional relationship with the business manager/fiscal officer is especially prudent.

Acceptance by Experienced Staff
Helps Newcomers Become "Insiders"

When considering the acculturation process, the principal new to a school will be well on his or her way to the insider stage if he or she can build trusting relationships with veteran staff members. Daresh (1993) estimates that principals new to their schools usually are accepted by the spring of their first year. Comments by seasoned teachers certainly will help newcomers gauge whether they are being accepted as insiders. If veterans say, "You're doing a good job," "You handled that situation well," "Thanks for that new idea," or "How about joining us for dinner?," then the principal is likely making progress. At the year-end faculty meeting, the principal might even feel free to comment, "Can you believe it, the school did not burn down under my leadership! Thanks for your support in making this happen."

CHAPTER 10

Balancing Leadership and Management

How can I begin teaching on Monday? I don't have enough student desks in my room.

A teacher preparing for opening day

It Is Risky to Separate Leadership From Management

Bennis's well-known quote, "Managers do things right and leaders do the right thing" (Bennis & Nanus, 1985), has a ring of surface accuracy. The quote suggests that a barrier can exist between managers and leaders with regard to their day-to-day objectives and long-range goals. Principals need to know that managers and leaders both do things right and do the right thing. A manager makes sure a schoolhouse remains clean because it creates a feeling of pride in one's school. A leader helps facilitate a curriculum team that selects the best resources for a school *and* makes sure that the resources arrive on time for the new school year.

Leadership literature frequently gives the impression that managerial functions or responsibilities are less important than the leadership functions or responsibilities. Principals usually want to be instructional leaders. However, management and leadership responsibilities go hand in hand. It can be misleading to separate the two responsibilities; it is more accurate to state that the managerial functions are subsumed within a principal's overall leadership responsibilities. A school principal noted, "The instructional leader also makes sure that the classroom lights are working." The converse also is true; ensuring that the classroom lights are working does not make one an instructional leader.

When a principal assumes leadership, it is critical that the curriculum objectives are in order. Yet, it is equally important that teachers feel that they have adequate resources available, accurate class lists, and schedules that work. On the first day of school, we want teachers to teach first-rate lessons. In addition, however, the bells must be accurately calibrated, there must be enough desks in the classrooms, there must be enough markers or chalk for the boards, and the electrical power and points must be operating satisfactorily for the new computer terminals.

Purposeful Visibility: Focusing On the Classroom as the Heart of a School

Another way of stressing how the management and leadership functions go hand in hand is by informing staff members and students that the heart of the school is the classroom, not the principal's office. Purposeful visibility (i.e., managing by wandering around) by circulating in classrooms, the hallway, the cafeteria, the gymnasium, and science and computer laboratories, as well as on the playground and around the bus area, will send the message that the principal does not "camp out" in the office but rather spends time in the various nerve centers of the school that are critical to an effective organization. The message should be clear: The most important place in a school, the heart of a school, is the classroom and other learning centers, not the principal's office. As a result, when principals visit classrooms to conduct teacher observations and watch students learn, the teachers and students will experience a greater comfort level because the visitor is a familiar classroom figure. A high school student spoke with one of the authors and recalled, somewhat humorously, a recent class in which he spent time that was unlike any previous class. The lesson was distinctively different. This lesson coincided with the unusual appearance of the school principal in the classroom. The student commented how he rarely saw the principal on campus. The student and instructor were struck by the event.

Successful Time Management: Proactive Scheduling to Observe Students in Action

Time management often is a dilemma for the principal. Gaining control of time is a challenge. One strategy is to block time on the daily schedule for walks around the school. For example, principals often schedule time to supervise students by the buses, walk through the halls, and eat with students in the lunchroom. They might select a different area each day and select a different time each day. By making sure that the secretary and teachers understand what they are doing, principals are simultaneously communicating an important message while spending time with students: Being accessible is important. One principal traditionally hangs a sign on her office doorknob during these times. It reads, "Out Learning."

This does not mean that each day you will be able to follow the schedule blocked on your calendar. Things certainly come up. However, you will be controlling your time to a greater degree. Moreover, you will feel good about your productivity and implementing your objective of purposeful visibility.

Time Management and Setting Goals

Most principals have grown up with the notion of "to do" lists. They get up in the morning and list what needs to be done that day. Or, if it is Saturday, they write down their chores for the day, where they will shop, what stops to make, and so on. Covey (1989) reminds us that although the "to do" list might seem like an efficient strategy, it really does not serve a long-range purpose unless the list includes items that are really important; that is, principals need to make sure that the bulk of their activities relate to their professional or personal goals. Principals must consider whether the "to do" list includes items that match their professional goals.

On the other hand, it is naive to assume that each day will run as expected. A school is not a corporation in which a chief executive officer (CEO) can set meetings and assume that, barring some major occurrence, everything will take place as planned. Schools, by their very nature, "invite" unpredictable events each day. A glitch in an assembly, a fight in the cafeteria, a disgruntled parent, a teacher-student disagreement, the district changing a curriculum plan, and the like can upset the daily flow of events. Because of the unpredictable nature of a school, it is imperative to keep one's eyes on key goals and priorities; otherwise, a principal often will experience control of time by others. Long-range time management that includes prescheduled blocking of classroom visits, time with students, parent meetings, celebrations of student work, teacher professional development activities, facilitating a curriculum meeting, walks with the custodian, and other important activities should be placed on a principal's schedule as a proactive strategy. Hence, although "things happen" that will upset the applecart, advance planning (based on priorities) gives the principal a good chance of accomplishing most goals. Again, the school secretary must be kept informed concerning the principal's goals. As part of a team, the secretary certainly can help the principal "massage" the schedule to meet the school goals and mirror the goals in his or her own behavior as well.

Seasons of Achievement: Managing
the Cycle of School Events

Another important time management technique is viewing the school year as a linear experience moving from one major period to the next, looking at each period as a season of achievement during the yearly cycle. Daly-Lewis (1987) refers to the cycle of events as "functional seasons." These seasonal activities might relate to the beginning of the year, the budget, various holidays, grading periods, standardized testing dates, professional development scheduling, curriculum reviews, parent events, special assemblies, extracurricular activities, academic achievement milestones, exhibitions and fairs, end-of-the-year events, and federal, state, and district reports. Activities will not creep up and surprise principals and teachers if a master calendar of activities is prominently displayed with copies distributed to all teachers. It also is invaluable for principals to keep hard copies and computer software files on these activities (often called "tickler files") as monthly reminders.

Following each season, principals should reflect on the activities and jot down their thoughts to improve the activity the following year. To avoid stagnation and increase creativity, principals should ask questions such as the following. Should we continue the activity next year? Should we create a new activity? How can we refine the activity? Are the activities meeting our overall school goals? An activity committee working with the principal can help to develop ideas and bring greater objectivity to this discussion.

The Formal and Informal Organization: Let's Get Things Done Around Here (Can We Cut the Red Tape?)

The principal often is seen as the standard bearer of the bureaucracy by the teachers and classified staff. The principal does things by the book, uses the proper forms and memos, follows the paper trail, documents, and so on. Initially, the principal should pay attention to the formal organizational chart, the specific job description, and traditional time lines. In reality, however, organizations usually deviate from the formal structures for those who are creative and innovative. An effective principal knows how to get things done quickly, cuts a couple of steps, and calls the right person at the right time. To do this, one must know how the informal organization works and who one can count on in what types of situations. For example, the principal needs to learn how to be polite yet persistent when dissatisfied with a response concerning an important request to improve teaching and learning for one's school.

The intent is not to break rules but rather to help the system work more productively. Principals should keep "mental notes" on the district office personnel who advocate strongly for students, develop informal relationships, and check with the effective and seasoned principals as well as veteran teachers in their schools to find out about the informal organization. Schools and district offices often are criticized for moving bureaucratically with top-down administrative structures. Using informal networks to cut the bureaucracy helps make the system work. One principal described the informal network as "the method through which information travels faster than the speed of any written memo."

For example, why is it that one school in a district (or one district in a state) has several computers in each classroom, whereas another school (or district) has almost nothing? The answer might relate to the resourcefulness of a principal or superintendent who knows how to procure what students need. The informal organization, in this case, might relate to networking with community leaders or a major computer company. The principal or district personnel know to which agencies to write grant proposals for computer resources and who are the best grant writers in the district. Principals need to use the informal network to learn this information.

Reducing Paper Use: Electronic Mail, Video Monitors, Memos, and Forms

The age of electronic mail (i.e., e-mail) might do more for the world's forests than formal organizations have done heretofore. As schools network administrators, teachers, and students through e-mail, fewer paper memos should appear each day. But, it remains to be seen whether e-mail will be a blessing, a curse, or both. On the one hand, the ease of e-mail lets us communicate immediately and frequently to a selected few or a whole group. On the other hand, as with hard copies, there is no guarantee that one will check e-mail messages, and the system can be used inappropriately by ambitious and "idea-a-minute" administrators and teachers who overload colleagues with too much information. Moreover, principals and teachers can easily fall into a pattern of sitting at their desks for an hour at a time answering 50 e-mail messages from colleagues. A few suggestions for principals to use e-mail effectively include the following:

1. Keep messages short and ask colleagues to do the same.
2. Do not feel compelled to read each message. Make a decision to read or delete messages after reading the headings.
3. Have the secretary scan e-mail messages to delete unimportant ones.
4. Try to read and respond to e-mail messages in one sitting. Do not worry if not all messages are reviewed. Critical correspondence should not be sent via e-mail.
5. Promote schoolwide electronic bulletin boards for selected topics so that each topic does not appear on everyone's system.
6. Do not use e-mail as a substitute for important one-on-one or group interactions.
7. Avoid using e-mail for confidential and sensitive topics. Security systems break down, and information can be misused.

8. Your e-mail address is as important as your phone number, so distribute it cautiously.

Hundreds of schools in the United States are using video monitors for morning broadcasts instead of the traditional public address announcement format. Training middle and high school students through broadcasting clubs can be an effective way in which to use this new technology. Using sophisticated technology that includes prerecorded videos, broadcast booths, canned music, video monitoring text only, and the like can make these informational sessions more appealing and build school pride. Although advanced technology might seem more appealing than using the traditional public address system, if the effort does not improve the traditional broadcasts or is intended for only a small part of the student body, then more efficient means should be used. More sophisticated technology should not be inserted as a communication tool just because it is there. Using available students to deliver messages to specific rooms and communicating via classroom telephones (if in each classroom) still might be the best methods to minimize disturbances. Furthermore, when it comes to morning and end-of-day announcements, consider that the brain remembers best what comes first and remembers next best what comes last. Given this, announcement times represent optimal learning opportunities. Is there something that can be taught during this time?

When distributing memo hard copies, paper waste should be reduced. Can the memo be reduced to only half a sheet? Can both sides be used? Can the memo be distributed to one grade level teacher and passed around without losing the message's effectiveness? If these practices are used by principals, then teachers are more likely to follow the example with their classes. Important messages about environmental consciousness are, in this way, communicated symbolically as business is conducted.

Concerning forms, when a newly hired principal begins, he or she should wait a few months before eliminating some of the traditional forms, always keeping an eye on system efficiency. When the principal is sure that a change should occur, then he or she should cut the red tape. The staff will appreciate the gesture. Each time a procedure is simplified and paperwork is minimized, teachers feel more professional. To illustrate, is it necessary to get a principal's permission each time a teacher needs to have something laminated?

Why can't a teacher receive, say, $300 for petty cash items for students during the year instead of requiring a completed form for every $4 spent? Questions like these should be raised by the administration in each school. The most reasonable answers might not always be easy to implement, but if at least a few changes can be made, then one has taken a step in the right direction.

Feeling Unprepared and Accepting the Notion: The Buck Stops Here

> You're responsible for everything. If some coach, when he's 50 or 100 miles away, screws up, you're responsible—because you're the boss. You're the one the parents get on. Or, if there's a problem, a conflict in the classroom, if a kid gets an "F"—they'll call you and want to know why. So, you've got to know, you've got to have your hand . . . on the pulse of the school.
>
> *A principal's voice*

Embracing the limited notion that school principals are trained to handle only certain "educational issues" (e.g., curriculum or scheduling issues) will leave one feeling unprepared, probably from the first day on the job. A principal should begin the job with the idea that hundreds of problems and challenges will appear on his or her plate that one cannot train for, anticipate, or predict. Each time a new problem or situation arises, even the veteran principal experiences the sense of being new on the job again. Having problem-solving strategies to cope with the unknown is a valuable resource. Using problem-solving strategies should become a general condition—a habit—when on the job. As noted earlier, Gorton and Snowden (1993) remind us that key problem-solving steps include identifying and prioritizing problems and challenges, determining possible negative consequences if handled improperly, setting deadlines for solving the problem, and using accurate sources of information about the problem. The results and deliberation period certainly will be different for most problems, but the basic process should remain the same.

Another key to coping with a feeling of unpreparedness is accepting Harry Truman's admonition that "the buck stops here." This does not mean that you know how to handle each situation or that you oppose delegating. It means that you accept responsibility for the school. Even if your school uses a site council, you still are responsible for implementing the decisions of that council. If a school bus breaks down on a field trip, you *can* tell the parents, "I can't believe how inefficient the bus maintenance crew is." But, is that an ethical approach? The parents certainly would be dissatisfied with your response. If a parent calls to complain about a standardized test, you *can* say, "I protested this type of testing to the superintendent." But, is that an ethical approach? Accepting the notion that the buck stops here ensures that you will accept responsibility for the school, that you will not be surprised by anything that comes your way, and that you will try to devise workable solutions. When interacting in sensitive situations, using empathy or taking the other person's perspective is a valuable communication tool.

The School Budget: Managing Finances and Resources

> The purpose of a budget is not to save money; rather, it is to help spend it wisely and expeditiously when needed.
>
> *Burrup (1977, Chapter 12)*

School budgetary responsibilities traditionally have been approached with anxiety by principals. A veteran practitioner described the budget process as having its own "mystic" of codes and operations that can be understood only after several years on the job. A principal's role as the financial administrator of a school site budget can vary from actively participating in developing and administering the budget as the school CEO to managing a budget developed in the central office.

Assuming that a principal has a moderate role in the budgetary process, he or she will be involved in planning, monitoring, administering, and cost control and accounting activities. At each stage of the school budgetary process, one works with teachers and classified staff members who advocate for their part of the budgetary pie, hopefully serving the best interests of the children. Budgets may be planned and calculated on paper with categories, codes, and dollars allocated, but they translate into human and material educational resources.

The bottom-line budgetary question regarding the resources should always be "How can the budget best serve the students?"

Leader as Learner of Budgetary Procedures

A principal new to a school should make an appointment with a district financial officer, a seasoned district principal known for his or her budgetary expertise, or (in smaller districts) the superintendent. The principal should politely ask the financial officer to review every major budgetary issue related to the school. To gain a broad and then specific understanding, the conversation with the financial officer should include the following questions or topics.

First, what are the major sources of revenue and actual dollar amounts budgeted for the school year for the district and the specific school to which you have been assigned? Sources of revenue in a specific school can vary depending on federal and state programs earmarked for specific student populations.

The primary source of revenue will be based on the apportioned state funding from average daily attendance (ADA) of students (also referred to as full-time equivalency [FTE]) based on specific days during the year. The ADA usually will dictate the number of teachers, classified staff members, administrators, and instructional resources for each school.

Special funding based on federal and state programs are a major school revenue source. The basic question to ask is "What is my school *entitled to* based on federal and state laws?" These sources provide money for students experiencing difficulty in reading, language arts, and math; vocational education students; bilingual education; migrant children; disabled children; at-risk children; gifted children; skills centers; community services, and so on. Funding for programs such as Title I, bilingual education, Head Start, and gifted education have become part of our educational vocabulary. Each principal needs to understand how these funds should be properly used.

Second, what are the budgetary categories and expected expenditures in actual dollar amounts for the district and your school? (A principal always is surprised to find out that approximately 80% to 85% of a budget goes to personnel expenditures.) Because the personnel budgetary allocations are basically out of a principal's hands, you should pay particular attention to instructional expenditures.

Third, compare budgeted revenues and expenditures for your school for the past 3 years. Ask the budget manager, seasoned principal, or superintendent to note line items in which the greatest discrepancy occurred between expected and actual budgetary expenditures. Discuss why these discrepancies developed.

Fourth, part of the intimidating mystic of a budget is related to coded numbers next to identified categories and dollars on specific budgetary lines. The accounting process looks daunting. It is not, but it does need review. Review the budgetary code for each expenditure on your school budget. How does the state and district identify and code items such as specific subject areas, textbooks, consumable books, athletic equipment, capital expenditures, software, high school items, middle school items, and specific federal programs? For example, items for the math department might begin in the "200" series, whereas those for social studies might begin with the "300" series. The coding system usually is logical and aligns with a specific master code list issued by the state and/or district. A principal does not have to memorize the coding system but must have the master code available, with allocations in each category, as expenditures arrive on his or her desk.

Fifth, ask the budget officer, principal, or superintendent to review categories that can be most confusing. For example, is there a district definition for a consumable workbook? Will the computer hardware be defined as capital expenditures or under a separate category reserved for technology? How are federal guidelines followed to "separate" a student receiving chapter funding from a student receiving migrant funding? With confusing categories, it might be best to work with another principal who has experience with the district guidelines. Although major decisions about federal funding might be made at the state or district level, a principal needs to know the rationale behind these decisions to effectively maximize the financial implications for the targeted (and sometimes untargeted) students.

Sixth, review the typical budgetary planning process and time line used in the district. In general, the planning process should include the following:

1. developing, with appropriate personnel, a preliminary budget;
2. justifying and submitting a final budget for approval;
3. approval of the budget by the board, often with changes;

4. administering and monitoring expenditures from allocated budget categories; and

5. evaluating allocated and actual budgetary expenditures.

The budgetary process is continuous and cyclical. As one is planning and administering the budget for 1 year, it is useful to consider how the financial decisions will affect the following year and what modifications will be necessary.

Districts have time lines for each budgetary step, and principals need to know and follow the time lines. Many districts have separate budgetary time lines for instructional and capital budget items. Specific preset dates for maintenance and service of capital items and facilities are budgetary decisions that usually are made at the district offices and finalized at board meetings. Principals need to pay close attention to these decisions to make sure that capital items and facilities are not neglected and school service and maintenance schedules are followed. For example, maintenance agreements for the copiers, language laboratory equipment, video monitors, and playground equipment must be adhered to because service agreements can be canceled with costly repairs if deadlines are missed.

Seventh, if the district has a curriculum review cycle, then carefully examine the cycle with the district financial officer and curriculum director (in the larger districts). Expenditures for the subject under review will greatly increase the year in which the review is completed because of the need to purchase new materials. Districts often follow 5- or 7-year cycles. Obviously, a 5-year cycle is more expensive and enables the district to purchase up-to-date resources more frequently. Some schools follow a 3-year technology plan to keep up with changes in this fast-moving field.

Site Councils and the Budgetary Plan

In some schools, site-based management has altered the ways in which schools make decisions. How actively central office staff members and principals work with teachers, parents, classified staff members, and community members at the school sites varies greatly. And the jury is still out regarding the effectiveness of the process. However, when teachers and administrators collaboratively work together on behalf of students, student achievement might be positively affected.

The days of holding the budget close to the vest are over. As one works with various stakeholders, it is important for principals to be open concerning how funding is decided. Even if a school is not practicing site-based management, active teacher participation along with parental input in budgeting decisions still is a prudent strategy—and one that builds trust and facilitates communication.

Associated Student Body Funds: The Potential Nightmare

Middle and high school principals typically state, "Teachers just do not want to take the time to carefully account for and document how student activity funds are used." Teachers typically state, "We are not hired to be accountants." Auditors indicate that the student activities budget can be the most irritating aspect of a school budget. They find discrepancies in student body funds because of insufficient documentation, shortfalls in funding, careless inventory accounting, inaccurate calculations, careless cash exchanges, and inappropriate use of funds. In almost all cases, these are honest errors. Yet, the problem can be serious because thousands of dollars might be involved for student association activities, sporting events, fund-raisers, yearbooks, clubs, activity cards, and so on.

The laundry list of advice regarding student funding includes the following:

1. accepting only exact-amount checks when admission is charged, such as for a ball game, to avoid giving cash as change from checks;
2. keeping funds in a school safe until open banking hours and depositing activity funds in a bank at the first opportunity after a social activity or sporting event;
3. constantly checking the inventory at student stores to minimize theft;
4. maintaining documentation with numbered tickets for events, keeping all receipts, purchase orders, and inventory records; and
5. maintaining up-to-date monthly and annual reports on the activity funds for the annual public budgetary presentation.

Also, one should network and develop a relationship with the appropriate district financial officer familiar with the activity funds. The principal needs to appoint conscientious staff members in charge of activity funding who enjoy working with students. The teachers, principal, and elected or appointed student activity officers should carefully follow the state or district activity funding guidelines (often published in an activity handbook for advisers).

Audits

Districts will be audited by the state on a regular schedule—and often unexpectedly. If an audit is scheduled, find out what usually is reviewed based on past practice to make sure that your records are in order. When the auditors visit the district office and review your school's records (or visit your specific school), use the auditing process to discover how to improve your school's budgeting, accounting, and documentation procedures.

Additional Budgetary Tips for Principals

1. Develop a strong relationship with the district financial officer. The colleague will appreciate your questions because greater accuracy of your school's accounting records will result.

2. Remind yourself that all budgetary decisions must reflect a commitment to students.

3. Fight for staff development funds in district and school budgets. They will enhance staff capacity to deliver a quality student instructional program.

4. Ask the appropriate school secretary and district financial officer to show you all forms that relate to financial issues. These include forms such as purchase orders, receipt books, petty cash vouchers, student body balance sheets, budgetary preparation forms, and cost estimate forms.

5. When teachers recommend purchasing an item (e.g., a microscope or laser disc player), find out whether the district inventories the item or uses a particular supplier with a set price. It is a waste of time searching for an item that the school district has on its supplier and price list.

6. When obtaining cost estimates from a supplier, always ask for a *written* estimate.

7. Keep your eyes and ears open for alternative funding for your school. For example, schools all over the United States have obtained computers below cost, and sometimes free, by writing grants or appealing to corporations or community businesses. In addition, educational grants sponsored by district, state, federal, corporate, or foundation sources can provide funding for a school. Major corporations in a school's area often provide grants as a community service and as a strategy to train potential employees for the corporation.

8. Explain financial decisions to the staff. More often than not, you will build trust and confidence with the faculty by making full disclosures while minimizing rumors regarding how money is spent. When a decision does not need to be confidential, it should be shared. Unnecessary confidentiality can be seen as a "power play" that indicates "I have information that I don't have to share with you because I am the boss."

Facility Management

> Orderly, clean buildings become statements of pride and reflect regard for students.
>
> *Sergiovanni (1992, p. 144)*

First impressions are critical and often lasting. The authors, over the years, have visited hundreds of schools. One can tell within the first few minutes of stepping into a school whether staff and students take pride in their facility. And the educational program is directly affected by the quality of the facility. Adequate lighting and efficiently operating science laboratory equipment affect students' opportunity to adequately complete work. Organizational charts might indicate that the district director of maintenance and operations and the school custodians are responsible for keeping the facility operating adequately. That information is accurate up to a point. However, as with every other aspect of the school program, the principal is the on-site CEO. The principal might not understand principles of electrical circuitry or how the heating system operates, but he or she is responsible for keeping the children warm. Again, Truman's admonition is applicable: "The buck stops here." It is important to know key maintenance people and build a relationship with them.

An inviting facility generates pride in a school on the part of the students, teachers, classified staff, parents, and community. Principals must ask the question: "What can I do to ensure that the physical plant generates community pride and serves the needs of students, teachers, and the community?" The following ideas, based on the authors' experiences and the recommendations of Hughes and Ubben (1989), cover critical suggestions to maintain a first-rate facility.

Maintaining the Safety and Beauty of the School Grounds

As a student or parent approaches a school, he or she sees how well the lawns, playgrounds, and exterior walls are preserved. Of course, if a school is in a city with minimal green areas, then well-preserved lawns might be unrealistic. That should not prevent an urban principal from having plants and gardens creatively cultivated around a school. Nor should it prevent a principal from ensuring that playground fences and equipment are maintained and attractive. There is no more disturbing sight than graffiti or broken windows as one approaches a school. Custodial staff members must remove graffiti and repair broken windows immediately for safety and appearance purposes. (If "evidence" is needed for disciplinary purposes, do not leave the mess; take a photograph.)

Playground areas should be kept safe and attractive. Equipment that is shoddy or a safety hazard might not only lead to an accident but could leave the school liable. It also is important that school grounds are well lit for evening activities and to reduce criminal acts.

Maintaining Safety and Beauty Inside a School

Just as a visitor gets a feel for a school by viewing the grounds, one immediately gains indicators of what is of value to a school when entering the building. A visitor should see clear, clean, and well-marked signs directing him or her to the office. Adequate lighting in the halls, well-placed trash cans, doormats, and a clean entrance are symbols of a school's pride and concern for visitors. Schools often have their mission statements prominently displayed for visitors. Examples of student work and important indicators of the school's tradition should be on display. Jane Foley, principal of Flint Lake Elementary School, placed the bell from the old Flint Lake School in a prominent place when the new facility opened to continue the school's traditions, history, and pride. When the new school opened, Foley (1996) notes, "We brought the whole school together to hear the bell rung by one of our teachers, who first rang the bell when he attended the original Flint Lake school" (p. 51).

One of the authors visited a public school on the Spokane Indian Reservation and was impressed with the quality and carefully organized displays of arts and crafts and historical portraits of Indian leaders that were prominently and proudly on display throughout the school. The facility generated pride in the community's history and reminds us how important it is to learn about cultural history and art. In addition to putting values on display, the inside of a school should be welcoming.

A Key to Facility Maintenance: Working Successfully With School and District Custodial Staff Members

Principals must recognize that they should treat all staff members, both certificated and classified, with equal respect. Moreover, principals should listen to what they say. This might sound like obvious advice, but it is important to listen sincerely and actively, provide adequate time for interaction, and display sensitivity to all staff members, both certificated and classified. Principals should set up regularly scheduled meetings with the head custodian and, on a regular basis, walk throughout the school (purposeful visibility) with the custodian to note needed repairs, celebrate work well done, and talk about what is important.

Depending on the time of the year, various issues should be discussed during meetings with custodial staff members. The daily maintenance routine of the custodial staff should be familiar to the principal and include frequent cleaning of halls and bathroom areas. Furthermore, long-range maintenance schedules and repair cycles developed at the district and school site level should be reviewed with the district director of maintenance and head school custodian. Depending on the district, the schedule might relate to items such as heating, air conditioning, lighting, copiers, student and faculty desks and chairs, carpets, shelving, doors, security systems, computer net-working, waxing, bell systems, painting, wiring, plumbing, sprinkler systems, phone systems, restroom equipment, physical education facilities, science laboratories, and roofing.

The principal should work with the head custodian to develop "user-friendly" forms for faculty members to report items that need to be maintained or fixed and to make sure the forms can be easily delivered to the custodian. In some schools, principals review all forms before sending them on to the custodian. That type of micro management probably is unnecessary unless telltale signs of inadequate daily maintenance (e.g., leaking faucets, sticky doors, broken windows) are observed by the principal, indicating that either the custodian is failing to follow a maintenance routine or faculty members have overlooked reporting maintenance needs. Maintenance forms probably should be delivered directly to the custodian, with the custodian reporting frequency and patterns of maintenance requests to the principal during their meetings. Summer maintenance forms, filled out by teachers and classified staff members, also should be used in a school. A teacher might notice a maintenance problem that had been neglected and overlooked or that should be moved up on the repair schedule (e.g., painting a classroom). These forms should be reviewed by the principal and custodian, with district input, to prioritize the summer maintenance work and to refurbish grounds and the facility.

Principal-Custodian Discussions on After-School Activities

The principal and head custodian meetings also should review after-school extracurricular and community activities. In larger middle and high schools, it would be helpful to have the athletic and activities directors attend these meetings. All principals have experienced the afternoon, evening, and weekend calls from groups that have shown up at school with the doors locked. (It can be embarrassing if the principal does not have the proper keys.) A copy of the extracurricular monthly calendar and community activity calendar should be prominently displayed in the head custodian's office just as it is displayed in or near a principal's office and in the athletic director's office. If adequate staffing is unavailable for after-school events, then the principal should pressure the district office to support custodial staffing for these events.

Those Snowy Days and the Bus Route

The miles of roads leading to and from a school are not literally part of the school facility. However, transportation safety on the route certainly is a principal's concern. Safety is especially an issue during snowstorms and ice storms when school districts must decide whether to cancel classes. Although it is not a pleasant task, in many school districts, superintendents, transportation directors, and principals travel the bus routes, sometimes at 4 a.m., to determine whether the roads are safe. Is this above and beyond a principal's duties? Individual principals have to determine this for themselves. When a parent complains that a bus route was safe and that school should have remained open, it sure is a lot easier for a principal to answer that parent by stating, "Mr. Smith, I appreciate your concern about your son's education and attending school each day. But I traveled that road at 4 a.m., and it just was not safe for our school buses."

The Teacher, Student, and Parent Role in Facility Maintenance

Part of taking pride in a school is taking responsibility for keeping the physical plant clean. Both teachers and students should work with the principal and custodians to keep the school clean. School rules need to emphasize the importance of sanitary bathrooms and using the school trash cans. The administration and teachers must be firm regarding vandalism including graffiti and locker damage. Art displays of paintings and photographs, prominently placed in a school, help to increase a facility's attractiveness and charm. Students, as part of their classes and as school service, certainly can help to maintain attractive plants and school gardens.

Active student involvement in recycling activities can send a strong message of reducing waste and keeping the campus clean of paper, cans, and bottles. Principals, modeling for students and faculty, should participate in scheduled activities that contribute to pride in the facility. Activities might include painting the school symbol in the gymnasium, creating banners for display outside of the auditorium, or organizing a display case of first-place photographs or pictures of distinguished alumni or students.

Parents, through the Parent-Teacher Association/Parent-Teacher Organization, booster clubs, or community organizations, can help to maintain pride in the facility. Raising money to improve, create, or build a playground area, an athletic field, a garden and plants, a lighting board, display cases, paintings, photographs, a statue of a school symbol, or even a bench can help to strengthen the school-parent link. Parents who are willing to volunteer to fix basketball rims, contribute the funds to buy paint, or volunteer to paint a school hallway feel a greater pride and a greater stake in their children's school.

CHAPTER 11

Expanding the Principal's Expertise: School Law, the Master Contract, and Grievance Strategies

I'm not an expert in the law, but I usually make good decisions because I have the legal manuals at my fingertips and know who to contact when a sticky situation occurs.

A principal's voice

Legal Relief

A course in School Law is essential for any student who desires to be certified as a principal. Moreover, common sense must be practiced even beyond requirements detailed in a state's public school manual. A principal must have the common sense to seek advice from principal colleagues and district legal experts regarding complex situations. (Lawyers working for a school district usually are available for consultation on key issues.) And although suspending a 6-year-old for kissing a classmate might not seem like a commonsense consequence, school administrators must protect the district and school

AUTHORS' NOTE: The authors thank Robert Iller of Whitworth College for his advice on the legal section of this chapter. We also thank G. K. Frizzel, a longtime Washington State school superintendent, for his help on the contract administration and grievance sections of this chapter.

by taking conservative actions in our very litigious society. (One should not forget that during the 1996 U.S. presidential election campaign, candidate Bob Dole received a call from a lawyer to sue the guilty party only minutes after falling off a platform in California.)

Interestingly, if you talk with several principals in a district, you will get varying views on how large a role law plays in their jobs. One year a school district might encounter few legal problems, and the next year an issue might "explode" because of a new state statute. Because of disciplinary problems, drugs, truancies, and more suspensions as students move up in grades, it is not surprising that middle and high school principals have more occasions to deal with legal issues than do their elementary school counterparts.

Legal Guidelines for School Principals

Regardless of grade level, there are some key principles and recommendations for school leaders that will help guide the newcomer whether he or she received an "A" or a "C" in School Law. These principles and recommendations include the following.

Practicing Due Process

The Fourteenth Amendment to the Constitution guarantees due process for all Americans. Due process is, of course, a fundamental American value and one of the most important principles of school law (*Goss v. Lopez*, 1975). And due process just plain makes sense. Legal proceedings that include an informal or a formal process are guaranteed to all students. This also applies to tenured teachers and, in some cases, to nontenured teachers if constitutional issues are involved (Aquila & Petzke, 1994). Regardless of grade level, students have a right to be heard regarding a disciplinary matter. The instinct to impose a consequence immediately to bring closure to a situation must be tempered by the requirement to talk to students about an infraction. If the infraction leads to a long-term student suspension or possibly expulsion, the formal nature of the hearing, of course, becomes more sophisticated. Principals must make sure that they check with key district personnel to ensure they have covered each procedural base regarding due process, time lines, and documentation expectations.

From a purely educational viewpoint, discussing infractions with students and their parents empowers everyone and helps to create a climate of community instead of confrontation.

Promoting Student Safety and Safe Equipment

Students love to run onto a playground and swing, slide, and hang from the athletic equipment. We must make sure that equipment is safe and that supervision is satisfactory. We subject ourselves to the potential of civil or even criminal negligence if students are placed in dangerous situations without basic supervision. According to Aquila and Petzke (1994), "The lion's share of negligence claims in the school setting involve allegations of failure to supervise students adequately" (p. 6). Safety regulations and, again, common sense make it clear that certain distances must be maintained around play areas and that safe and soft landing areas should be maintained in proximity to all playground equipment.

Furthermore, trained adult supervision should be close enough so that if a student falls and breaks an arm, an adult is immediately available to assist. If a parent hears that his or her child broke an arm without prompt assistance, then that parent has a right to be angry. Although the degree of supervision might not be as comprehensive for older students, supervision still must be present. This is especially true for athletic activities whether they are practices or actual games. Personnel might include spotters for gymnastics or qualified first aid personnel for any athletic activity. Principals should work closely with custodians, playground personnel, and coaches to make sure that students use only safe equipment and that supervision is constant, with help available immediately. Emergency numbers should be posted on or near phones to save precious minutes in an emergency. Supervisory personnel should be briefed on strategies to control and console crowds in the event of an emergency.

To avoid accusations of negligence, it would be prudent for school leaders to ask the following questions:

1. What foreseeable risks may be involved in this particular activity?
2. Is it possible to eliminate or reduce the risks by the exercise of ordinary care?

3. If it is not possible to eliminate or reduce the possibility of risk, would it be prudent to eliminate the activity? (Iller, 1996a, pp. 3-4)

Documentation of Important Events

Documentation is a necessity in a variety of situations. For example, in the preceding discussion of school safety, it is important for comprehensive documentation to take place if a student injury or an employee injury occurs. One never knows when the documentation will be needed. Furthermore, every important meeting with a parent or teacher concerning a student should be documented. Certainly, if a student suspension or expulsion is imminent, then documentation of previous incidents will substantiate one's "case" and indicate that a concern has existed previously. Time, date, setting, and a summary of the dialogue should be noted as well as any written documents used during the meeting.

Parents (and the student) have a right to see the documentation in the child's file. The tricky part occurs when we want to keep personal notes for our own use and to refresh our memories in addition to the "official" documentation that may be used for a legal proceeding. It is difficult to give advice on how to handle this issue because one never knows how courts may decide in the future. It probably would be safe to advise that one should keep the official documentation objective and descriptive, including only information that one could share with others.

A child's future school has a right to know about official documentation relating to serious disciplinary infractions. Educators frequently withhold disciplinary records when a student transfers schools so that the student can "turn over a new leaf" without prior records inhibiting his or her reputation. However, "In the world of the 1990s, this in no longer a viable option. In court, the judge's expectation is that you *knew* or *should have known* alerting information which could have resulted in more appropriate monitoring of potentially dangerous behavior" (Association of Washington School Principals, 1996, p. 2, emphases in original). Moreover, when records are released for a student transfer, confidentiality and security must be maintained.

In addition, schools have to be very careful about releasing student medical information. Because of AIDS and other medical issues, parents are concerned that their children will be stigmatized if too many school personnel know about their difficulties. For example, in some states, student medical information can be released only with parental permission through a school-authorized nurse to specific administrators and teachers.

Following Time Lines

Principals must stay informed regarding time lines and deadlines for a variety of due process situations. Missing the deadlines usually means losing the particular "case" on a technicality. For example, if a grievance is filed by a teacher, the education association or union master contract usually has a grievance procedure with time lines that need to be followed as the grievance moves from the principal, to the district office, to the school board. If nonrenewal of a teacher contract is in the works, then notification of the school district's intent needs to occur by a particular date, a period of assistance outlined (usually for tenured staff members) with notification dates for nonrenewal with appeal procedures. For a student suspension or expulsions, district time lines usually need to be followed for due process hearings before the suspension or expulsion occurs unless a student's continued presence in school entails an immediate danger to the student, other students, and/or school personnel or a substantial disruption to the educational process.

A Proactive Hiring Practice: Following Up Teacher Recommendations

To follow up the due process issue, one of the most time-consuming and unpleasant responsibilities of a principalship is dismissal of a teacher. The process can occupy almost all of a principal's time when the issue comes to a head. As a proactive and preventive measure, it is crucial to thoroughly follow up written recommendations for a prospective teacher with phone calls to administrators and, if possible, a visit to the prospective teacher's school before hiring. The legal quagmire of firing a teacher, especially if the teacher has tenure, can be circumvented or avoided if efficient hiring procedures are used.

Having a Colleague Present
During Key Meetings

If a sensitive meeting concerning a school issue needs to occur with students, teachers, or parents, then the principal should consider having a colleague present. In the case of a grievance by a teacher, the union representative always should be there. Of course, in some cases this might not be practical (e.g., if a parent privately wants to tell the principal about a recent divorce). Furthermore, if the principal feels that he or she will be verbally attacked or if the individual calling the meeting might be unstable, then one should not try to be a hero and handle the meeting on one's own. In a serious incident involving disciplining of a student, the presence of other adults should be considered. Also, by having a "witness" present, the principal will have someone with whom to reflect concerning the dynamics of the meeting.

Knowing the Community

Legal problems can occur for a principal when he or she is unfamiliar with the culture of a community. For example, Halloween recently has been under scrutiny in many communities as promoting "devils and witches." Whether a principal wants to fight the battle over Halloween might depend on the mood of the community. Is it a free speech issue? A curriculum issue? Is it better just to ask teachers to have "harvest festivals" to avoid a battle? Faculty dress, particular books in a library, certain films, and how the curriculum is taught all are issues that might not raise an eyebrow in one community yet might raise the roof in another. Principals should consult with veteran staff members to find out whether a "battle" is likely so that one is prepared to handle the possible repercussions and plan proactively.

Maximizing Opportunities for
Students With Disabilities

The law of the land stipulates that all students, regardless of their degrees of disability, have a right to a free and appropriate public education. The Individuals with Disabilities Education Act of 1990 (IDEA) provides federal financial assistance to state and local educational agencies to ensure that all disabled students who fall within 13 specifically defined categories (e.g., mental retardation, orthopedic impairment) receive "free, appropriate public education" with guaranteed procedures to ensure that education. The Rehabilitation Act of 1973, Section 504, prevents discrimination against students with any disabilities in all programs and activities receiving federal financial assistance. Examples of Section 504 handicapped conditions not covered by the 13 categories specified in the IDEA legislation include disabilities such as HIV, asthma, allergies, attention deficit disorder, behavioral difficulties, and temporary medical problems. Principals need to know these laws well and especially the strategies and recommendations that have resulted from the IDEA statutes. Areas of particular importance include statutes relating to disciplinary issues and Individualized Educational Program (IEP) requirements such as expectations, program review, funding options, and related services (e.g., speech pathology, accessibility to facilities) (Aquila & Petzke, 1994).

In short, IDEA provides funding and procedures (e.g., a specific IEP plan and team) for disabled students who fall within specifically defined categories of disabilities. Section 504 protects a broader range of students who need special services but does not ensure funding for these students. It also might be valuable to subscribe to publications, such as the journal produced by the Council of Exceptional Children, to become aware of recent laws and cutting-edge practices to support these children.

Title IX and the Guarantee of Equal Educational Opportunities for Males and Females

In 1972, the federal government abolished discrimination based on sex of any educational program or activity receiving federal funding. This act has forever altered the landscape concerning opportunities and expectations for female students and ensures that they receive the same or equally opportunistic programs and activities. Specifically, the act prohibits sexual discrimination regarding admission, recruitment, course offerings, counseling, marital or parental status, activities, and athletics (Aquila & Petzke, 1994).

Schools and the public have noticed the changes foremost in the area of athletics, whereby female students must be provided with competition, equipment, supplies, scheduling, traveling, coaching, academic tutoring, facilities, training, and publicity equal to those of their male counterparts. Students growing up and going to schools today can barely notice a difference in opportunities; however, the changes in the past 30 years clearly indicate that previously we were headed in the wrong direction, denying female students the equal opportunities that are a birthright of each American.

As noted previously, Title IX also covers course offerings, counseling, and other aspects directly related to the academic program. Principals must make a conscious effort to safeguard the academic opportunities of their female students. Of particular concern is the underrepresentation of females in math and science classes. For example, middle school principals must work with teachers if female students are not appropriately represented in the algebra and science sections for the "advanced" eighth-graders. High school principals need to keep abreast of the upper level math and science classes and ask the appropriate questions if female enrollment is lower than male enrollment in these classes. Conversely, if males are not represented adequately in the upper level English classes, then questions should be raised. Although it might be difficult to prove that practices related to enrollment in academic sections are based on sexual discrimination, a principal can be a strong moral voice in a school supporting the spirit of Title IX legislation.

Search and Seizure

School principals are not law enforcement officials and are not held to the same standard as are police officers. When conducting a search to investigate a disciplinary incident, the doctrine of *reasonable cause* (or reasonable suspicion) applies to school leaders, whereas the doctrine of *probable cause,* a higher standard for a search, is applicable for law officers. In the case of *New Jersey v. TLO* (1985), the U.S. Supreme Court stated that *"reasonable grounds* for suspecting that the search will reveal evidence that the student violated either the law or the rules of the school" provide school officials with the right to search a student under their jurisdiction. However, it is important that school officials limit the search based on the circumstances and recognize that "the greater the police involvement, the higher the standard required to justify the search" (Iller, 1996b, pp. 2-3).

Remain Current Concerning the Law

It is important that principals remain current regarding important legal decisions and school procedures affected by the decisions. Almost every major principalship journal has a monthly section on school law. In addition, it would be prudent for principals to attend law workshops sponsored by national and state principal organizations and individual school districts. During these next few years, we probably can expect some important court decisions regarding Internet use and free speech relating to schools.

Remaining current concerning legal issues is essential as new laws are tested in each state. At times, the federal government or a state legislature passes a law without considering the ramifications of the law for the individual schools. For example, in Washington State, the legislature passed a law in 1995 that was intended to reduce student truancies. The effect on individual middle and high schools was considerable in terms of the paperwork that ensued to keep up with students who were not attending schools. It remains to be seen whether the legislation will make a difference. Principals need to network with one another, the district, and state officials to find out how to cope with new policies. Certainly, we still are experimenting with strategies to successfully implement IDEA legislation. Unquestionably, principals will develop better strategies in response to new laws, the more we network and share our successful (and unsuccessful) practices. In the meantime, making school a meaningful and inviting experience can serve, in some cases, to reduce the peril of truancies.

Making Sure That District and School Site Policies, Regulations, and Rules Align With the Law

When a rookie or seasoned principal accepts a new position, it is essential to familiarize oneself with the district policies and individual school handbooks regarding a school's philosophy and mission as well as policies concerning discipline, attendance, and academic expectations. In addition, a newcomer needs to know district policies and union contracts concerning certified and classified staff. It is impossible to memorize all of the specific information in these manuals, but a general feeling for the essence and intent of the documents is helpful. All the policy manuals, rules, and regulations must align with federal, state, and municipal statues. If a principal is unsure about the legal status of a policy, then he or she should check with district personnel to clarify whether the policy is in compliance with the law.

Have Federal, State, and Municipal Statutes Readily Available

Again, it is impossible for most principals to memorize all the important statutes applicable to schools in any state. Even if a principal successfully memorizes each statute, that is no guarantee that he or she will do the right thing when a legal problem occurs. Yet, it is important that relevant laws are in one's office, and, when necessary, a principal should know how to easily find a law. When a legal interpretation is needed, a principal should have no reservations about calling a principal colleague or district lawyer for advice.

Administering the Master Contract

> It amazes me how many times a grievance occurs because a principal did not read the contract.
>
> *A local teachers' union president*

Although school principals are not directly involved in creating the master teaching contract, they are responsible for administering that contract in a school. An effective principal cannot lament about the strengths and weaknesses of a contract—or how he or she could have produced a "better" contract to serve the needs of students. The primary purpose of the contract is to protect and benefit teachers. The principal must accept the contract, "warts" and all, and maximize the effectiveness of that contract to best serve students, teachers, and the teachers' association or union.

When the topic of unions or teacher associations is discussed among principals, one often gets the idea that the relationship can only be discussed in "we/they" terms—as a relationship always in conflict. Principals expecting "trouble" from teachers' associations might find their principalship beginning on the wrong foot if they do not operate on the premise that teachers and administrators have a common objective—to work together in the best interests of the children. Furthermore, it is important that principals recognize the history of the teachers' unions in education as a movement that developed in the 1950s and 1960s to protect teacher employees and obtain due process, better working conditions, and honorable salaries. In general, these objectives have been obtained. According to the late Albert Shanker, former president of the American Federation of Teachers, confrontational tactics no longer are necessary because teachers today have a voice (Checkley, 1996).

Know the Contract

Probably the best advice or strategy for all principals is to know the master contract better than the teachers know it. This is not to outwit teachers but rather because principals should avoid slipping up on simple teacher contract rights and procedures. To implement this proactive strategy, principals should meet in the district office before the school year begins to review contract language (or a new master contract if just negotiated) with appropriate district personnel or veteran principals. To prepare for the meeting, principals should review the contract language and note sections that are ambiguous. These noted sections should be raised as issues with scenarios studied, possibly with role-playing, to help with proactively planning for conflicts that might arise. Remember, the leader is a learner, and learning about the nuances of a contract is an appropriate learning opportunity. Certainly, principals will be familiar with some aspects of the contract from their years as teachers or administrators. This is especially true for the many principals who played active union roles before choosing administrative careers.

Continued networking is essential. Find out who the most successful principals, district personnel, and district lawyers are when working on union and master contract issues. Follow their advice on critical issues. A local union president suggested to the authors that principals should contact the teachers' association for clarification on an issue from a union viewpoint. Why not? Although this might not seem like a prudent approach from a traditional viewpoint, if we are creating new alliances, then this strategy might help to build a bond, reduce communication problems, and empower the union as a source of information in a new collaborative working relationship.

Developing a Relationship With
Union Representatives in the Building

It is very important to develop a trusting relationship with the building representative of the union. Set up a regular meeting with the representative, possibly biweekly or more frequently if necessary. Ideally, there should be no surprises on either side. A strong bond between the principal and union representative will help the school through the difficult times. Union leaders often are experienced staff members, very savvy, and very political, and their insights can be invaluable to principals. By working with the union representative, a mutual understanding can be worked out to deal with a situation uncomfortable for both sides. Interestingly, when a teacher in a given situation is a "thorn in the side" of the principal, the teacher might also be a thorn in the side of the union. Furthermore, if the literature on the "new union" is accurate (*Education Update*, 1996), then principals should work with union representatives on staff development and reform possibilities to enhance collaboration and teacher empowerment in curriculum and instruction.

Grievances and the School Principal

A grievance is defined by the *American Heritage Dictionary* as an "actual or supposed circumstance regarded as just cause for protest" (Houghton Mifflin, 1976, p. 579) relating to a *possible* violation of the master teacher contract or of state or federal law. Keep in mind that a grievance does not firmly establish that a violation occurred. The grievance procedure will determine whether a violation occurred by examining the facts. Any teacher in the union may file an individual grievance. Also, a class action may be filed in which one plaintiff, or a group, files a grievance on behalf of an entire school or district.

Why Are Grievances Filed?

The school principal represents the school district as the chief administrator of the collective bargaining agreement in each school.

The principal will interpret the master contract and will face grievances when he or she implements an action that is interpreted by the teachers as a violation of the contract. In the same district, there might be several principals who have very different "success" ratios with the union or teacher association. For example, Kaiser (1995, p. 211, citing the work of Johnson) notes that in one New York State school district with 11 schools, more than half of the district grievances were filed against one principal. As noted previously, the number of grievances filed against a particular principal might tell us little about a principal's effectiveness. The principal with the most grievances filed might simply be taking a stand on issues that previously have been swept under the carpet or taking a stand on issues that he or she feels need to be examined to improve student learning.

Possible reasons for filing a school grievance include the following:

1. The principal is unfamiliar with the contract and constantly is asking teachers to take inappropriate actions.
2. The principal is not following stated time lines to avoid grievance procedures.
3. The union or building representative is very powerful in the building and a stickler about contract language.
4. One teacher, for various reasons, is the catalyst for several grievances.
5. The union is setting the stage for the next collective bargaining agreement and filing grievances to test the waters.
6. The principal is "encouraging" grievances to bring an issue to light.
7. Past practice is being tested, for example, a practice that has become acceptable but is not in the contract such as teachers arriving 5 minutes before classes begin in the morning.

The Purpose and Stages of a Grievance Procedure

A grievance procedure includes several steps that are carefully worded in the master contract. The procedure usually guarantees the right of appeal until arbitration and prohibits unilateral resolution of the grievance. Each step has been carefully crafted to maximize the satisfactory resolution of the grievance. Normally, the steps will proceed from appeal to one's immediate supervisor (usually the principal), to the district superintendent, to the board of education, to arbitration.

If the grievance is not resolved informally with the immediate supervisor, then each stage usually will include the following:

1. a written explanation of the grievance by the aggrieved party or the grievant's representative;
2. a time line for both sides to follow to prepare for hearings;
3. subsequent hearings to provide the information developed by both sides;
4. a written decision (following the time line) by the district administrative representative after the hearing; and
5. the arbitration stage in which both parties are bound to accept the arbitrator's decision, made within specific time lines (the decision usually becomes part of the public record).

Avoiding the "Snowball Effect"

An issue that initially seems minor can turn into a major school or district grievance. Two or three upset teachers can snowball an issue into a major school or district conflict. This can result because of several reasons. First, the principal might be taking the conflict or grievance personally and feel that he or she needs to stand firm. This can be a self-created "trap" for a principal trying to assert himself or herself. A principal must remember to separate a teacher from the teachers' union when a conflict occurs. As noted previously, it is essential to find out whether the issue is really important by checking with other principals in the district or with district personnel.

Second, morale in a school can be low for various reasons, and a spark created by any source can lead to a major conflict. For example, although a master contract may specify how long faculty meetings should last, a grievance should not result if two or three meetings extend a few minutes past that time limit. However, if a school is experiencing low morale, then it might not take very much effort by a principal to "push the buttons" of the faculty. Strictly following a master contract on such a minor issue might seem unimportant, but it would be prudent to follow procedures until one gains a faculty's trust and has a good understanding of a school's culture.

Grievances as a "Safety Valve"

It is important to keep in mind that the grievance procedure was established to provide a legitimate means of complaining about a circumstance that appears unjust. The grievance can prevent a "spark from becoming the Chicago fire" (Frizzel, 1995). This is a major reason why one should reject the notion that a filed grievance is a personal attack. To avoid a major "fire," a principal should stick to the grievance facts and interpret the situation as an opportunity to clarify a perceived injustice. The grievance might help to clarify contract language and improve working conditions.

General Advice for Avoiding and/or Handling Grievances

The following advice concerning grievances is based on the personal experiences of the authors and suggestions by Frizzel (1995), Gorton (1980), and Kaiser (1995):

1. Daily concern for the working condition of teachers is an essential proactive strategy to minimize the number of grievances.

2. A principal's relationship with the building union representative can be the most critical factor concerning the number of grievances filed and the resolution of grievances at the building level. Work to make the relationship a collaborative one characterized by trust and understanding.

3. A principal should tell a teacher to consider bringing the union representative to a meeting if the principal thinks the meeting might raise problems concerning the master contract, leading to a possible grievance.

4. A principal and district administrators need to know and follow the specific time lines or deadlines for each grievance step. Failure to follow the time lines will result in the loss of the grievance by the school district.

5. A principal always should remain approachable regarding a conflict that might develop into a grievance. Remaining approachable includes respecting the grievance procedure

system, remaining courteous, taking the initiative when setting grievance appointments, arriving promptly for meetings, and following through on commitments.

6. During grievance meetings, the principal should remain a good listener, seek clarification, and try to determine the facts that are agreed on by both sides.

7. The principal should take notes during grievance meetings for later reflection and reference.

8. When meeting with the aggrieved party, the principal should not negotiate an agreement on the spot or impulsively make a decision, even if the principal is sure about what needs to be stated regarding the grievance. A decision must be made thoughtfully, with care, and within the time line stated in the master contract. The principal must inform and discuss the decision with his or her immediate supervisor or district administrative representative responsible for handling grievances before sharing the decision with the aggrieved party.

9. After reviewing a grievance and following the time line, if a grievance is to be denied, then it usually is prudent for a principal to simply write "grievance denied" (if that is permissible) on the initial form before it is appealed to the next level.

10. As much as possible, the decision should be presented to the aggrieved party without any indication that personal feelings have become an issue.

11. A school principal is employed by a school district and can be directed by the superintendent or school board to deny a grievance at the school level. The principal must accept and fully enforce the superintendent's decision. It is important that the principal does not send the message, "This was not my decision. I'm only doing what I was told." This message implies that a principal is unwilling to take responsibility for a decision. Also, it can diminish, in the mind of the aggrieved party, the legitimacy of the next step in the appeal process. It is quite possible that the superintendent or school board simply needs time to check with contract specialists so that a fair decision can be rendered.

Teachers as a School's Greatest Resource to Help Students

Finally, it is essential to constantly keep in mind that teachers are the principal's greatest resource to help students reach their potential. A traditional management versus employee relationship does not make sense in a schoolhouse where the management and employees are working hand in hand to assist students. Moreover, a traditional autocratic relationship with teachers is counterproductive in this era of empowerment and democratic leadership. It simply does not make sense to alienate teachers when the educational goals of principals and teachers are the same.

CHAPTER 12

Implementing a Proactive Behavioral Program

Students need to feel safe in order to take intellectual risks.

Kohn (1996, p. 103)

To develop a comprehensive and effective approach to school discipline, the school as an ecosystem concept again becomes an important notion to consider. A proactive and effective approach to school discipline must be holistic, involving good instruction, responsibility-centered disciplinary strategies, violence prevention and security options, student activities, pupil guidance services, and partnerships with the community.

There are few aspects of a school program that receive more attention than the behavioral system. A quick way for anyone to evaluate a school is to simply walk around a school and observe the classrooms, cafeteria, and other areas and make a judgment as to whether the school is safe and a good place to learn. Rookie or veteran principals new to a site might be apprehensive about the code of conduct and the behavioral expectations in the school. They know that many teachers, students, and parents will judge their initial success based on how they alone, or with their assistant principals, will handle discipline.

When a principal is hired, he or she moves into a school that likely has in place a behavioral program with established policies. The program could be based on a variety of strategies, ranging from behaviorist interventions to a more cooperative and community-building approach. The behavioral program can include a multitude of words, terms, and strategies such as punishments, rewards, rights and responsibilities, logical consequences, praise, mediation, decision making, catching kids being good, time out, coercion, creating community, detention, suspension, and expulsion. The same terms will have different meanings and will be used in strategically different ways by various teachers and administrators. One teacher might perceive rewarding students for acting properly as a sound classroom management strategy. Kohn (1996) would disagree: "The promise of a reward is sometimes not just ineffective but counterproductive, that is, worse than doing nothing at all" (p. 33).

A principal might have strong feelings about whether a school is going in the right or wrong direction with its disciplinary policy. This chapter provides a range of ideas to develop a comprehensive and proactive behavioral program that should help a principal evaluate his or her school's approach to discipline. However, one should not assume that there is a fail-safe formula for each school or classroom. As Kohn (1996) reminds us in *Beyond Discipline,* "It's disrespectful to teachers when someone proposes to replace their judgment with a packaged response. Moreover, prefabricated interventions are rarely useful for getting to the bottom of problems since they usually turn out to be ways of punishing or otherwise controlling students" (p. 122). Kohn suggested that school personnel consider helping students with skills and opportunities to make good decisions, build community instead of competitive environments, improve the quality of school rules, develop tasks to help students flourish, provide students with authentic choices and responsibilities, and minimize classroom restrictions (e.g., Is sharpening one's pencil a major privilege?).

Good Instruction: The Most Effective Proactive Behavioral Strategy

The most powerful and successful way in which to reduce disciplinary problems is to provide meaningful instruction that interests students in caring classrooms. When students in caring and productive classrooms are working on worthwhile tasks, they are less likely to cause difficulties. A key aspect of this approach is forging strong relationships with the students. The popular expression, "People don't care what you know until they know that you care," certainly applies to most students and adults. A school principal should be concerned when faculty meetings and staff time constantly are preoccupied with finding better disciplinary strategies rather than discussions about effective instructional strategies, curriculum, student motivation, and building relationships with at-risk students.

It would be naive to state that classroom and school disciplinary strategies and codes of conduct are not critical; they are. But an effective behavioral approach is part of good teaching. Helping a teacher become a better teacher is a primary way in which to reduce disciplinary problems. Heller (1996) reminds us, "Appropriate school discipline must be a part of every program, curriculum, and practice . . . through both instructional and non-instructional programs" (p. 2).

Responsibility-Centered Behavioral Strategies

School principals spend years as teachers in classrooms and have strong views on how students should behave. The authors' experiences in the classroom and the principalship led us to the following definition of classroom management: "Effective classroom management is the conscious use of proactive strategies and procedures to help students behave in a way to provide maximum learning opportunities for each student in the class. Through such a management system, students are encouraged to develop skills for self-discipline" (Robbins & Alvy, 1995, p. 228). Key questions for principals to ask include the following. Are we preparing students to behave without constant teacher supervision? Are we preparing students to take ownership of their behavior? Have we successfully communicated to teachers our support when they take risks to encourage student autonomy?

Kohn (1996) maintains that effective teachers help students become enabling, autonomous, and effective independent decision makers. These teachers model collaboration, care about and take an interest in their students, and work to create respectful and trusting classroom communities that offer students choices. The use of punishment, coercion, or rewards is rare. Kohn indicated that successful relationships with students, in which they self-learn appropriate behaviors, help make children ethical people with moral meanings to their lives.

When an elementary school teacher uses stickers as a reward, is he or she preparing students to take ownership of their behavior? When a newly hired principal enters a school, he or she might feel strongly about immediately changing the policy of rewards and punishments, but it probably is prudent to wait on the changes. Why should the faculty trust the advice of this "unproven" newcomer? A longtime superintendent reminded the authors that even if a new principal strongly disagrees with the way in which things are going, "You almost have to do it their way first." Another superintendent gave advice by modifying a carpenter's old adage, "Measure twice, cut once; you only have one school." Why? First, you need to see how the system works; your "theories" might not be appropriate for the setting. Second, by immediately changing the system, the principal is failing to honor and respect the decisions of others. Even Kohn (1996) is cautious: "In short, change, particularly a revolutionary change such as this one [moving from rewards and punishments], must be made gradually, respectfully, and collaboratively" (p. 142). Remember, the principal is modeling a behavior. If one is going to suggest working with students in a more collaborative way, then one should model that behavior with faculty if disciplinary strategies need changing.

As a principal new to a building, you are likely to take over a school with a behavioral system that is based on rewards and punishments. You must first be convinced that a different approach to discipline makes sense before you embark on a challenging expedition that might dramatically affect how administrators, teachers, and students interact. The use of time outs, suspensions, expulsions, rewards, and stickers is part of the system, and making changes—possibly significant ones—will take a lot of convincing. What works in one setting might not work, and might not be appropriate, in another setting.

Zero Tolerance Policies

There are some disciplinary expectations on which a principal should not compromise even if the principal is unsure regarding his or her philosophy on rewards and punishments. For example, schools must have a zero tolerance policy regarding violence. Burke and Herbert (1996), the principal and vice principal, respectively, of a large urban high school, maintain that their school's decision to implement a zero tolerance policy reduced the number of violent incidents from 195 during the 1990-1991 school year to 4 during the 1992-1993 school year. They affirmed the message of zero tolerance: "Foss [High School] administrators suggested to the faculty that it was time to adopt a dramatic new policy: Fights would no longer be tolerated. 'If you fight, you will no longer be enrolled as a Foss High School student.' This simple but effective intervention was whole-heartedly accepted by the staff" (pp. 50-51). The administration communicated the policy to everyone. The policy was posted in every classroom, announced weekly on the public address system, emphasized in parent and school newsletters, and stressed during orientation programs and opening-day assemblies. "The one-year anniversary of the zero tolerance policy was celebrated by an assembly and skit about continuing expectations" (p. 52).

Developing Proactive Behavioral Guidelines

The approach taken by Burke and Herbert (1996) is a good example of addressing the *specific* problem of school violence. It also is important to review *general* strategies to develop schoolwide disciplinary guidelines appropriate for a particular setting. When developing disciplinary guidelines, consider the following:

1. State the guidelines positively and with clarity. A list of "don'ts" sets a negative tone.
2. Except when absolutely necessary (see Guideline 3), avoid guidelines that are too specific. Consider general principles that would include specific offenses.
3. Guidelines that should be absolutely specific should include the right to undisturbed teaching and learning; total intolerance [zero tolerance] for physical violence and drugs; hurtful, sexual, or racist language; academic dishonesty; and vandalism.
4. If you are not sure that a particular guideline can be enforced or is the responsibility of the school, consider leaving the guideline out (e.g., students are not permitted to smoke within three blocks of the school).
5. Safety should be a prime consideration when developing guidelines. A school must first be safe.

6. If students can be involved in developing guidelines, their commitment will increase; however, remember that student responsibilities go along with student rights.

7. All guidelines should have a rational basis. "It has always been a rule" is not good enough.

8. School rules should align with the school mission.

9. School rules must reflect district, state, and federal legal statutes. (Robbins & Alvy, 1995, pp. 223-224).

Violence Prevention: A Crisis Plan and Security Options

A Crisis Plan

The term *proactive* has no greater application than when a school develops a plan for violence prevention. There are some very simple and commonsense measures that every school should take to protect students and staff. Armistead (1996) provides some excellent suggestions for principals beginning with the importance of developing credibility before a crisis occurs. Part of this credibility rests on developing a ready crisis prevention plan. The plan should include information on who will speak for the school, how the faculty and district office will be notified, how students will be kept informed and cared for during a crisis, ready and feasible evacuation plans, a coding system for faculty and staff concerning crisis situations (e.g., two bells indicates an intruder, so classroom doors should be locked), where the information center will be located, health service personnel, medical services (especially trauma unit personnel), clergy, key parents, the media, a telephone tree, sample letters to parents, and a telephone list of key personnel from the fire and police agencies and the bomb squad.

Protocols to respond to violent incidents or other emergencies should be part of an emergency procedure manual and include steps and strategies to cope with drug overdoses, kidnappings, weapons violations, shootings, severe violence, racially initiated violence, bomb scares, and deaths (sometimes sudden and traumatic) to staff members, students, or parents. The plan also should include commonsense ideas such as having one press conference instead of speaking separately with 10 reporters and making sure that parents are notified about traumatic events before the media are notified. Armistead (1996) stresses, "After the gunshots are fired is no time to figure out who will speak for the school or to look up phone numbers for the local news media so you can share important information with your community" (p. 32). Armistead also reminds us that a parent's first question always will be, "Is my child safe at the school?"

Again, the pupil guidance service personnel can be a helpful source when developing protocols. Training faculty members and students in CPR and first aid procedures can save lives and reduce injuries. This type of training also will help to build loyalty and community in a school. The message is clear: "We are in this together." Older students, especially those in high school, can be consulted for ideas and strategies when emergency manuals are developed. Traditional drills to test procedures are critical.

Security Measures

Heller (1996) recommends using the expertise of fire and police agency personnel to do a security review for a school. "This may involve a review of the school's lighting, parking, security staff and procedures, alarm systems, and general procedures related to open and ongoing communications with the local police and fire authorities" (p. 4). Although a school should be an accessible institution welcoming a community through its gates, a school also must cautiously and responsibly monitor visitors to protect students, faculty, and staff. Visitors should be directed to clearly marked entrances with only one or two entrances available during the school day. Security measures in some areas dictate that all visitors must "sign in" during the day. In some schools, there are distinct guidelines for visitors. In one school, for example, former students returning to visit staff members are welcomed on campus only after 3:30 p.m.

A coding system for faculty and staff should be enforced when confronting a questionable intruder. The system should include specific steps for visually signaling other staff members and verbally communicating with the intruder to reduce the possibility of a tragic incident. Unfortunately, many schools have found it necessary to tag faculty and students with photo identification as a security measure. All security actions and policies should be communicated clearly and frequently to students, faculty, staff, parents, and the broader community. The message must be firm: The school is going to be a safe place for students. Again, security experts from the police and other agencies should be involved in developing these policies.

The Student Activities Program

When students take pride and feel good about their school, they are less likely to cause problems. A key way in which to feel good about a school is to be involved in worthwhile school activities. Hill (1996) focuses on safe school solutions, stressing the importance of helping students make responsible decisions by participating in the development of classroom rules, engaging in town meetings, and serving on site-based teams. She also stresses that having students learn CPR and first aid can increase their sensitivity to one another and increase their value of human life. Hill notes that service learning has become institutionalized in almost 50% of U.S. schools.

Service learning, becoming involved in the community, helps students feel that they are making a contribution to the community while developing civic pride. Service learning includes helping senior citizens, getting involved in environmental projects, assisting the homeless, teaching adults to read, teaching others how to use technology, assisting in classrooms, and helping with the Special Olympics, Big Brothers, and Big Sisters. "At some middle and high schools, students, along with teachers, serve poor children in the neighborhood every week. They share snacks with the children, teach them health habits, tell stories, watch videos, and enjoy one another" (Robbins & Alvy, 1995, p. 222).

Johnson and Johnson (1996) stress the importance of conflict resolution activities for students. These programs can be with cadres of students or with a whole school. The programs teach mediation, decision-making, problem-solving, and negotiation skills. Johnson and Johnson maintain that conflict management strategies are successful because "every child and adolescent needs to learn to manage their conflicts constructively. . . . The more years students are taught how to manage conflicts constructively, the more likely students are to maintain the use of the procedures and skills" (p. 17).

Heller (1996), a school principal in New York, mentions other interventions that serve as proactive activities. These include anger management seminars that teach strategies to deal with anger (especially for students who have been involved in fights), the Partners

Acting as Instructional Resources program that pairs faculty members with at-risk students, and peer mediation programs that train students as mediators (p. 6). These programs, as well as the conflict resolution programs, are excellent examples of getting students involved and teaching practical skills.

The traditional student activities program of sports, music, drama, student newspapers, yearbook, and other clubs helps provide a "glue" for a school while building community. Students involved in these activities look forward to school and take pride in their contributions. Student activity success provides faculty members with an opportunity to see students succeed in endeavors that might be in sharp contrast to classroom performance. This can be a very refreshing and positive experience for faculty, administrators, parents, and students. Other typical school activities, some yearly and others on occasion, include Model United Nations, student government, jazz club, ecology and recycling club, science and technology club, art club, broadcasting club, chess club, school service club (e.g., helping in homes for the elderly or with the visually impaired, disabled children, or tutoring), Future Farmers of America, foreign language club, Key Club, student store, ethnic club, student-teacher assembly planning club (e.g., Spirit Days), glee club, creative writing and/or poetry club, electrician club, and Earth Day committee. The possibilities for clubs are limitless, and each time that students attend club activities, they are in healthy, productive, cooperative situations that increase their loyalty to a school and offer collaborative opportunities to interact with teachers, classified staff members, and/or community volunteers.

Pupil Guidance Services

A proactive behavioral program relies considerably on a first-rate guidance program. For example, when a new student enters a school, counselors can be a positive initial contact for the child and parents to let them know that this school is safe and part of a caring community. The counselors can help new students make initial contact with classmates so that they do not feel like strangers. Through a guidance counselor's intervention, a peer support group of students can assign each new student with a veteran school classmate. A counselor's intervention can be a make-or-break opportunity with an at-risk student entering a new school. "Counseling is one of the most effective forms of prevention/intervention techniques for those students with behavioral or academic problems" (Adami & Norton, 1996, pp. 22-23).

As with all leaders, effective counselors are visible in a school with students, parents, teachers, and administrators. They also help to develop curriculum for community building. The curriculum is used to design middle school advisory periods for intramurals, discussions, class business, tutoring, service projects, and school-to-work career options. Counselors often receive staff development training in conflict mediation, peer mediation, and decision making to train the faculty to share these techniques and skills with students. Their skills as individual or group counselors and as advocates for disabled students, their role in child study teams, and their general availability—just being there—when a student cries for help can significantly contribute to a school's tone of caring for students.

Counselors can be very helpful in developing assessment tools and recording data to keep track of at-risk youngsters. Many counselors have strong assessment backgrounds and can assist the administration with the management of records of suspensions, truancies, drug and alcohol use, grades, tardies, class cutting, weapons, and violent acts. Because these data are critical to the guidance program, counselors can develop strategies to work with teachers, administrators, parents, and community resources to reduce these unhealthy school statistics. These statistics must be addressed openly and honestly. Yearly reviews of these data let schools know whether they are making progress on the disciplinary front, especially when new intervention strategies are tested.

Counselors can help to develop needs assessment surveys and/or action research projects to secure feedback on student, faculty, and community morale. These surveys can probe for answers to questions such as the following. What do you like best about your high school? What can the school do to improve your high school experience? Students, teachers, and parents could be surveyed on topics relating to academics, homework, activities, communication, and the school's reputation. These assessment activities provide general opportunities to be part of the decision-making process and make suggestions to help the school become a better place, especially for students and staff. Again, these data could assist counselors, administrators, and teachers with their school improvement efforts. Counselors should be actively involved in creating and assessing school disciplinary codes at the district and school levels. Counselors can provide important input because of their training, especially with regard to the long-range consequences of a policy.

Partnerships With the Community

Networking with public and private community-based organizations (CBOs) is another critical role for school counselors and administrators. Counselors and administrators should have the names of these community contacts on index cards or in a computer database. These organizations can provide resources and assistance to help at-risk youngsters in and out of school. CBOs can offer skill and intervention training to help students in their academic programs and school-to-work transitions. Typical organizations can be health centers, social service agencies (some located in the school), religious groups, neighborhood associations, women's centers, universities, youth centers, art organizations, museums, business partnerships, YMCAs, merchant associations, American Legion, Kiwanis, Lions, drug and alcohol rehabilitation centers, sports associations, liaison assistance from the police department, child welfare organizations, United Way, job placement agencies, Drug Abuse Resistance Education (DARE), Mothers Against Drunk Drivers (MADD), Big Brothers, and Big Sisters.

It is important for school staff members to review data about their students and determine which organizations might be able to support school-level efforts on behalf of these children. For example, depending on the student and family situation, the following services are available in large urban centers and, at times, in rural districts: programs to assist students dropping out of school, support for first-time youthful offenders, college scholarships, parenting training, nutrition awareness, homework assistance, child care while parents are at school conferences, breakfast and lunch programs, domestic violence and conflict mediation for individuals or families, assistance for disabled youngsters, general equivalency diploma programs for parents, consumer training, assistance for pregnant minors, and retired individuals willing to serve as mentors.

Some Final Thoughts on
Approaching School Discipline

Because of medical developments including MRI technology, we now know a lot more about how the human brain works. Medical research tells us that, when under stress, the brain actually "downshifts" (Caine & Caine, 1991) and that, when angry, we often can exercise little control over our behavior (Goleman, 1995). Beyond the research data, Kohn (1996) logically suggests that the more we use inflexible disciplinary measures and provide students with few opportunities to make decisions, the harder it is for students to "become morally sophisticated people who think for themselves and care about others" (p. 62). One principal in Allentown, Pennsylvania, provides a quiet place for students to "cool down" and ponder their behavior when they are sent to her office because of infractions. She regularly educates students in the office and in the classrooms about their brains, their behavior, and the importance of resisting impulsivity.

Interestingly, anyone who prepares for the principalship studies the work of Douglas McGregor and his leadership Theories X and Y. Theory X suggests that if we assume that humans dislike work and cannot be trusted, then we have to coerce them and threaten punishment to get results. With Theory X, humans are by nature irresponsible and must be directed to get work accomplished. By contrast, Theory Y suggests that humans can be trusted and self-directed when committed to an idea. When a leader believes that workers can be trusted, the workers will be more creative and self-directed (McGregor, 1960). The application of Theory Y for a school's behavioral policy is obvious. If we expect students to become more autonomous and self-directed, then we need to provide them with opportunities. Principals set the tone for this autonomy in how they relate to faculty and staff and in how much support they are willing to provide teachers and counselors in their work with students.

It is important to consider the social context of a behavioral policy as well. One of the most difficult aspects of the principalship is balancing how we want to treat an individual with what is best for a school. How many times have principals thought to themselves or shared privately with colleagues, "It's too bad that it was Sally who broke the rule, but we need to be consistent when reinforcing rules"? Choosing between what is best for an individual and what is best for a school can be a distressing dilemma. It is important to be consistent. The image of the whole student body looking on when a decision is made certainly creates a vision that encourages consistency. However, as seasoned principals know, there are times when rules need to be broken. That might be a confusing bit of advice. But as principals construct their administrative visions and focus on how they will advocate for children, knowing when to break the rules may, at times, become a necessary choice.

The Structure and Culture of Schools

Many educational reformers take the position that until we are willing to change the structure of our schools, little progress can be made to reduce disciplinary problems, student violence, and academic failure. Structural and cultural examples that minimize success include teacher isolation, middle and high school teachers seeing more than 150 students daily because of traditional scheduling, and overcrowded elementary, middle, and high school facilities. These are critical ideas to consider when restructuring how we do things in our schools. Some larger middle and high schools have divided their buildings into family groups, houses, divisions, or teams (i.e., schools within schools) in which teachers, administrators, and students work more closely together to get to know one another better in this context than in the larger, more impersonal setting. Smaller schools seem to work. The oft-cited example of the Central Park East Schools in Manhattan, New York, probably is one of the best known success stories of how schools can be organized into smaller and more successful divisions in which the administrators, teachers, and students know one another and work together toward a mission focused on building community, collaboration, and student achievement (House, 1996).

In this same context, Linda Darling-Hammond, co-director of the National Center for Restructuring Education, Schools, and Teaching, reports,

> Growing research evidence illustrates the success of alternative organizational arrangements—smaller, more communitarian structures fostering more cooperative modes of learning, less departmentalization and tracking, a more common curriculum for students, stronger relationships between teachers and students that extend over multiple years, greater use of team teaching, and participation of parents, teachers, and students in making decisions

about schooling. . . . This participation appears to be most productive when schools create many opportunities for developing
shared knowledge among teachers, administrators, parents, and
community members and when they create joint work in which
this knowledge can be used and deepened. (Darling-Hammond,
1996, p. 13)

Many of these alternative organizational possibilities can be implemented in most schools with creative, dedicated, and sensible
leadership and deliberate and honest discussions with faculty and
parents about the possibilities. It is important to see the relationship
among different aspects of a behavioral policy such as good teaching,
proactive disciplinary strategies, an effective guidance program, and
healthy school activities. This brings us back to the notion of the
school as an ecosystem dependent on various components interacting for student success. Darling-Hammond's (1996) description of
productive schools certainly aligns with this notion.

Spending Time With Students

Principals should interact with students in a very personable
manner to demonstrate the principal's role in the ecosystem in building a sense of school community. Some principals greet students as
they get off the bus every morning. A principal reflected,

This simple act has multiple meanings. It may represent the first
kind words a kid has heard and give him a boost for the day. It
allows me to connect with kids in a different light. It also gives
me a pulse of the community for the day . . . [and] helps me anticipate possible things that may arise.

Other principals hand out breakfasts and lunches, play sports, "hang
out" during passing times, attend sports games, and read to classes
to accomplish similar objectives.

Finally, the importance of good teaching and a sound curriculum
cannot be overemphasized. Our most successful teachers have fewer
behavioral problems, not because they are tough disciplinarians but
rather because they are good teachers who work hard and integrate
decisions relating to curriculum, instructional strategies, and individual
student experiences and assessment in a meaningful context that ex-
cites and engages students.

CHAPTER 13

A Principal's Vision for Teaching and Learning

You have to believe in yourself and what you're trying to accomplish . . . and you have to hang in there with your goals. . . . I'm extremely goal-oriented and can look far enough ahead so I can see it is going to take me 10 steps to that goal. . . . Eventually, I'm going to get there.

A principal's voice

One of the most emphasized leadership ideas in recent years is the importance of vision and developing a focus—"seeing" the school mission. A vision can be perceived from an organizational or individual view. An organizational vision most often emerges as a consequence of a process in which organizational members take part. The leader's role in the organization is to help shape the vision and then assist in maintaining and keeping the organization focused on the vision. Creating a school vision through consensus is a very complicated and challenging responsibility. Teachers, although working in the same school, traditionally have closed their doors and conducted their teaching as if they were in separate little schoolhouses with separate visions—and often distinctly different philosophies. If teachers are to "link" their classrooms, then they need to feel there is a worthwhile cause to do so. To a great extent, the value of a school-wide vision depends on the quality of the process that a faculty and community goes through in developing the vision.

An important activity for a leader is to develop an individual vision, a vision of courage to help one keep in mind what is important. Principals, reading in business and educational journals about "the vision thing" and having the idea emphasized during educational administration courses, still might be unsure about school visions or maintaining their own visions of leadership. Ironically, even if schools have firm mission statements, principals can feel "lost" if they are not sure how to proceed as school leaders—how to translate and implement those missions into visions of leadership. Questions that emerge as they reflect on such leadership visions include the following. What should be the school's key commitments? What issues should I have the courage to stand up for? When should I compromise? How can I best communicate the important commitments to students, faculty, parents, and community members? Revisiting the vision in light of recent activities, accomplishments, and behaviors is essential to determine whether it is driving the organization and its members or whether mid-course corrections are warranted.

A Vision of Clarity

Hearing someone else's vision sometimes can be helpful in forming one's own ideas. One of the authors attended a seminar on building school and community relationships and heard a very clear vision. The seminar was for administrative interns studying to be principals. During the seminar, ideas were shared concerning a community leader's perception of how a successful principal should operate.

The seminar focused on building relationships in a new school made up of students from several old and traditional communities of various ethnic groups. An African American community pastor, Happy Watkins, talked about the success of the school during the second year. The school's first year was very controversial, partially because of distrust among different ethnic communities. The distrust made it very difficult for successful communication to occur between the school and the community. The pastor thought that a leading reason for the success of the school during the second year was the appointment of the veteran but newly hired principal, Alison Olzendam.

When describing the principal's success, Watkins indicated that the principal was fair and recognized that racism was categorically unacceptable. Then he added, "Each of you as an administrator can make a difference. Be fair and expect the best" (Watkins & Olzendam, 1996). Watkins' vision was quite clear. As the seminar progressed, he gave examples of fairness (e.g., making sure that gifted programs were open to students of color) and indicated how disappointing it was to see a local symphony with few people of color. The pastor firmly stated, "It just wasn't fair." Although his remarks focused on fairness and expectations for all students, certainly the comments about fairness can be extended to anyone affiliated with a school whether a student, a teacher, a classified worker, a parent, or a community member. This was a vision that a school principal certainly can follow.

A Long-Range Vision

Hall and Mani's (1992) description of "strategic sense," a long-range vision, is a powerful theme for a rookie principal: "Those principals who were able to keep in mind their longer term goals, and the themes that they were developing to get there, were able to do more and with greater coherency and greater pulling together on the part of the school staff" (p. 60). Strategic sense might be what makes or breaks a principal's success. Strategic sense certainly refers to a principal's own professional focus on successful teaching and learning and building a sense of community through creative leadership. The suggestion by Hall and Mani that early identification of a vision, strategic sense, enabled these newcomers "to do more" should strongly motivate all principals to clarify their philosophies and educational goals.

A principal's voice:

You really have to be a strong person. You have to have a certain strength in you, a certain commitment to kids, and a commitment to education—particularly a commitment to kids, to rise above the kind of nit-picking and back-stabbing and so on.

Right from the start, it is important to have a vision and "press the accelerator"—but not too fast. This is one of the paradoxes of the principalship cited by Deal and Peterson (1994). On the one hand, we have said to go slow, be flexible, be patient, and not push too quickly toward a particular agenda. On the other hand, the principal is expected to move quickly, focus on a mission, walk and talk the mission, and implement change. The changes may include specific goals such as creating a safer school while reducing suspensions or increasing professional development about authentic assessment. The changes may embrace more general goals such as reemphasizing the commitment to children and doing our best to help children reach their potentials. Let us not forget that teachers, although anxious, expect newly hired principals to implement some changes. It is just human nature to expect newcomers to introduce new ideas. Echoing Deal and Peterson's paradox of the principalship, Hart (1993) suggests that principals should "forge ahead" with changes yet "recognize the limits of their influence on schools and take heart in small changes" (p. 210).

Keeping the Vision Systemic

If one envisions the school as an ecosystem, a systemic view implies the importance of considering all of the components of a school and their relationship to meeting school goals. To realize an instructional vision, one must consider the relationships between and among various components—the formal and informal school structure, curriculum and instructional expectations, and faculty professional development options.

The Formal and Informal Structures

A principal must look at the structure of the whole organization and consider how the various components or parts of that structure contribute to, or inhibit, collaboration and community among students, faculty, parents, administrators, and the external community. For example, if we accept the notion that successful schools are places in which teachers interact about teaching and learning and take shared responsibility for students, then we need to ask, "Is the school structured to enhance such interaction?" A principal's vision of how that interaction can be realized can enhance the possibilities of this becoming a reality. Formal structures might not be created to facilitate dialogue, so the leadership might want to restructure the "organizational lines" to meet the needs of students and faculty. For example, a principal can structure faculty meetings to exchange ideas, organize workshops on topics of interest to staff members, and encourage faculty members to share ideas after returning from a conference. One principal offered a faculty member the services of a school secretary to prepare a report. Another asked technology staff members to help develop a presentation using the PowerPoint™ software program.

The traditional factory model of management does not focus on the role and impact of the community (external forces) on the school system (Hoy & Miskel, 1996). Formal structural arrangements leave little room for ideas such as school-based management or school improvement teams that include parents and community members. (One has to be careful about making the site-based councils too formal or else they, too, can become another layer in the bureaucracy.) A principal viewing the school as an ecosystem can envision how each force or component can have a positive or negative effect on the school. Consider how a school can benefit from developing a partnership with a local business such as a supermarket. High school students can learn how stores market merchandise, monitor products, hire and fire, organize the accounting procedures, and train staff members. An effective partnership can flourish by inviting supermarket employees into the school to share information, and the school art class might contribute drawings, artwork, or sculptures to enhance the supermarket's lobby or entrance.

A traditionally structured school is a closed system operating within strict boundaries. The structure inhibits a school's ability to gain constructive feedback from the parent community. Logic would dictate that a traditionally structured school would conduct all parent meetings in the school. Watkins, the pastor, believed that Alison Olzendam was the right principal for the school. Alison tossed out the formal structure and conducted informal parent meetings in the community. She called specific parents, asked them to conduct meetings in their homes and the community, and asked the parents to invite 10 to 15 other parents to share parental views on the school's strengths and areas in need of improvement. Alison had a vision of community involvement that dictated reaching out and seeking feedback in an informal, nontraditional manner to create a more balanced school ecosystem.

Other examples of a traditional and formal structure include the 50-minute class period, traditional textbooks, formal disciplinary procedures and punishments, traditional hiring practices, most teacher evaluation systems, separate academic disciplines, separate grade levels, tracking, and traditional tests. It would be easy to dictate a list of informal structural examples and imply that traditional and formal structures are "bad," whereas progressive and informal ones are "good." This would be naive and unfair. It is important to consider how to make connections between formal and informal structures to meet the specific contextual needs of students and adults in schools and communities. Informal structures do not exist until they are created. When a vision emerges, it usually fosters the development of informal structures that reflect that vision.

Using Informal Strategies to Move From the Formal and Traditional Master Schedule

Many schools have used a decision-making matrix to study master schedule options to best address their needs. These options range from the traditional 50-minute class period to various block schedule arrangements. First, the matrix is aligned to list important scheduling *considerations* along the vertical axis (Figure 13.1). For example, the schedule must provide opportunities for an existing inclusive practices program to continue. Or, the program must provide several class options among which the students may choose. Next the considerations are weighted according to their importance, with *very important* receiving a 3, *somewhat important* receiving a 2, and so on.

The horizontal axis is where programs under consideration are listed. Then, each program is rated according to the degree to which it meets or exceeds the consideration. Ultimately, when the scores are tallied, it becomes evident which program best addresses the needs. Making data-based decisions using staff input not only enhances the chances that the choice will be the right one but also builds respect, credibility, and communication, all of which are valuable for successful leadership.

The Curriculum and Instructional Leader: Fine-Tuning the Vision

No problem can be solved from the same consciousness that created it. We must learn to see the world anew.

Albert Einstein

Consideration	Traditional 50 Minutes	4 × 4 Block	8 Block	Modified Block
Sufficient variety of classes (3 points)	____ X3	____ X3	____ X3	____ X3
Opportunity for advanced placement students (2 points)	____ X2	____ X2	____ X2	____ X2
Inclusive practices (3 points)	____ X3	____ X3	____ X3	____ X3
Teacher availability (2 points)	____ X2	____ X2	____ X2	____ X2

Figure 13.1. Decision-Making Scheduling Matrix

Although there are disagreements in our society concerning how schools should operate, how teachers should teach, and what should be taught, there is little disagreement that the world is a very different place today than it was 100 years ago. Historians suggest that the skills of a worker of 2,000 years ago could very well have been sufficient until barely the last 100 years. The nature of jobs is changing even more rapidly today. Naisbett (1982), in *Megatrends*, estimates that most workers will change careers three times before they retire and that successful executives will make five career changes. Drucker (1992) notes that until the mid-1970s, unskilled blue-collar workers dominated the job market; by the year 2010, they will constitute only 5% of the market. "Now a majority of the new high-paying jobs are in knowledge work: technicians, professionals, specialists of all kinds, managers" (p. 131). Drucker stresses that business has given way to the knowledge society: "The center of gravity has shifted to the knowledge worker" (p. 5). And Drucker is concerned that schools, right through to universities, are not teaching vital organizational skills such as expressing ideas orally and in writing, collaborating effectively with others, and shaping one's work and career. As school leaders, principals need to recognize these changes in the job market and the implications for schooling.

The explosion of information technologies means that individuals who know how to gain information likely will have the edge in the schoolhouse and workplace. Ten years ago, a home encyclopedia, school, and the neighborhood library were considered the critical sources for seeking information. Today, anyone with a computer at home, in school, or in the workplace has more information available through the Internet than does a scholar working through the stacks in the Library of Congress. Consequently, we are literally going through a revolution concerning the quantity and availability of information. The answers are there for the taking. The question remains "What is worth knowing?"

The revolution in technology certainly has altered how we gather information. However, that revolution has not altered the basic democratic goals of schools. America has been involved in a 200-year experiment that has attempted to educate for excellence and equality. The "American Dream" is that citizens should get an equal chance through public schooling and learn how to practice democracy. Visionary school leaders expect all students to succeed. Interestingly, the high school graduation rate in the United States is more than 80%. Yet, as a nation and as school leaders, we are not satisfied with that percentage—one of the highest in the world—because the American Dream carries the expectation that everyone will graduate. As a cautionary note, one needs to recognize that technology can increase inequalities among schools and students if the wealthier schools have more technology and better trained technology teachers.

Considering the American Dream and the changes in the workplace, school principals and teachers must keep schools relevant to prepare students for responsible citizenship and employment. Deciding what is relevant can be an abstract notion unless we bring it home—literally. One university professor asks each student in an educational administration class to consider the following scenario:

> You have the opportunity to send your own child, or the child of a friend or relative whom you love very much, to a school you will create. The premise of the activity is that all educators, including all principals, should provide the same opportunities for each child in their schools that they want for their own children. To expect anything less is unethical and immoral. The four questions that need to be answered in the scenario are as follows:
>
> 1. What characteristics would you like for your child's teacher?
> 2. What types of activities/strategies should be used in class?

3. What are the important subjects/content areas that you would like your child to learn?

4. What would you hope to see when walking in the school?

As a principal prepares for a new appointment, it is helpful to reflect and answer these questions. The answers should include examining what one knows as a consumer of research on teaching and learning and one's intuitive thoughts about outstanding teaching (and learning) based on personal experience as a student and observations of other teachers. Following are a few examples.

1. What characteristics would you like for your child's teacher?[1]

We want our children to have a teacher who cares deeply for his or her students, even loves them and expects them to "reach for the stars." The teacher should be approachable for parents and should ask parents about their children's interests and follow through on the ideas that emerge from this dialogue. The teacher should be bright and have a good core knowledge of the curriculum and child development and should use various strategies to teach, depending on the strengths of each child. It is important that the teacher is serious about learning (e.g., he or she does not waste time and monitors work) but has a good sense of humor and helps the students to feel comfortable in class. Comfort is really important, and we hope that the teacher creates a climate in which the children are comfortable with making mistakes; students should feel comfortable raising their hands when a question arises.

It is important that our children's teacher is a lifelong learner. The teacher should be reflective and build on her craft knowledge based on experiences and exchanging ideas about teaching and learning with other experienced staff members. By the way, longtime experience is not critical. The enthusiasm and energy of a first-year teacher is valuable. We hope that the teacher continues to engage in staff development opportunities and has the dedication to experiment with a strategy (e.g., performance assessment) recently studied.

2. What types of activities/strategies should be used in class?

We would like to see students working on various projects— short- and long-range ones—that give one a feeling of adventure, discovery, and accomplishment. The projects might include the building of a model bridge, creating a map showing a pioneer trail, performing a class play, writing a book of poems, or conducting a science experiment over several days. Clearly, we would like to see hands-on strategies, math manipulatives, technology multimedia projects, and opportunities to present orally to the class. We think that it is important to see our children reading quietly at times using both fiction and nonfiction sources, acquiring a taste for a broad range of literature, and working on complex mathematics work. It would be a pleasure to hear quiet music playing in the room when the students are writing.

On the other hand, we would expect to see a lot of cooperation and teamwork, with students helping one another and freely exchanging ideas. As the teacher plans lessons, we would hope that he or she uses the experiences of our children and lets them construct personal meanings as they learn important curricular content. It also is important that the teacher does not feel restricted about spending a particular amount of time on each lesson. Some activities might take 10 minutes, others 2 hours or 2 days. There should be a joy as students learn during each activity, with the teacher helping to arouse their curiosity by creating a climate for decision making and problem solving in which the students see the activities as important, not just facts to be memorized for the next test. The effect of the teacher's strategies should lead to a love of learning as our children would look forward with anticipation to continuing a project.

Formal testing in the class should not be a dominant activity. We would hope that traditional paper-and-pencil tests with lower level questions would be very infrequent. Although we would be interested in how our children performed on a standardized test of reading, our method of judging reading success is more likely to rely on a request at home; if we received requests from our children to "stay up late" to continue reading a book, then we would declare the reading program a success.

It is important that our children use performance and authentic assessments and have an opportunity to share, at length, what they know. We hope that our children will be preparing portfolios during the year and that our teacher conferences include portfolios to see our children progress during the year. Upon visiting the class, it would be reassuring to see student work on the walls. In fact, we would not mind ducking to avoid contact with mobiles hanging from the ceiling.

3. What are the important subjects/content areas that you would like your child to learn?

We want our children to learn the basics, but we would not create a hierarchy of subjects that suggest "This is more important than that." However, our list of basics is considerable and includes reading, writing, oral expression, math, technology, social studies, science, art, music, physical education, and foreign language. As our children study these subjects, it is important that connections are made and that subjects are not perceived as separated from each other because we think it is important to "soften the boundaries between traditional subject areas" (Ahlgren & Kesidou, 1995, p. 44). The complexity of ideas should be addressed; memorization of facts might work for school tests, but the real world is more challenging. In the world of work, writing is not separated from reading or an oral discussion about the possibility of a dam failing during a flood. Thus, thematic and integrated learning should connect the various disciplines. Furthermore, the disciplines should not be perceived as subjects taught "with a finish line." The subjects should be taught as part of a journey that will last a lifetime. We hope that the teacher will develop an expertise in questioning to address the complexity of ideas and arouse our children to think both logically and creatively.

Concerning the specific content of each basic subject, we hope that the teacher has reviewed the work of the major associations as they have developed their "standards" documents. For example, by examining the National Council of Teachers of Mathematics (NCTM) standards, we would hope that the teacher makes interdisciplinary connections and uses communication, logical reasoning, and real-life situations to teach problem solving, computation, communication, geometry, probability, and statistics. Certainly, the emphasis of each subject area (e.g., geometry) will depend on grade level, but it is important for the teacher—whether elementary, middle, or high school—to have a broad conceptual understanding of the disciplines and the disciplinary connections.

We want our children to learn to read from a variety of fiction and nonfiction sources, especially complete works, and to develop an appreciation of multiethnic and multicultural literature. We are concerned that television, video machines, and movies are a strong magnet for our children, so it is critical that they find passion for books and reading as well. We would like our children to develop a love of writing and have frequent opportunities to write creatively, and we believe that the writing process that emphasizes prewriting activities, drafts, peer reviews, editing, and publication is an effective strategy. Certainly, we do not expect that with each writing activity, our children will go through every stage of the writing process, but it is important that our children do not fear writing because they are afraid the teacher will find too many spelling or grammatical errors. We want our children to have experiences with various modes of writing, from formal reports to personal and private expression. For example, daily journal writing would be welcome. The ability to express oneself orally, with comfort, in an organized way also is critical.

Social studies should provide our children with a curiosity about government, history, economics, current events, other cultures, and an appreciation of the American experiment. Teaching social studies only as facts would be unfortunate for our children because there are rich opportunities for learning. For example, role-playing activities can combine history with economics as students develop a plan to travel west on the Oregon Trail. Learning to read a newspaper and understanding the cause and effect of events are important activities for our children. Cause and effect also should be emphasized in helping students to acquire knowledge of the past and how the past affects present events. Learning to appreciate other cultures through interdisciplinary activities combining literature, history, music, and art can be facilitated through the social studies. The social studies also can be the springboard for building collaboration and community through class and school student government. Developing a civic awareness is important as well.

Science education should pursue the goals of "Project 2061" (American Association for the Advancement of Science, 1990) with an emphasis on science literacy and the interdependence of math, science, and technology. Both physical and life sciences should be addressed, with a strong emphasis on hands-on experiments, field trips, and integration of science into everyday life. We hope that early exposure to science will stimulate interest in biology, geology, chemistry, physics, and astronomy. Understanding and using the scientific method as a critical process for objective study should be emphasized. The importance of systems, and the interdependence of things, is critical throughout the science curriculum and provides an excellent forum for integration with the social sciences through heredity and cultures. The integration should raise consciousness about ecological issues and science's impact on society.

We would like our children to receive foreign language instruction from an early age. Most children pick up languages easily if they are taught early enough. Also, the instruction should have a strong cultural component and help students develop positive values about other people and nations.

We believe that art, music, and physical education are "basics" because for some children it is through these disciplines that talents are discovered. It is tragic when great musicians, artists, and athletes are not discovered because children did not have an opportunity to "find" and explore their talents. We hope that this does not happen and that our children will gain an appreciation of the fine and performing arts.

We want our children to get a heavy dose of technology because it will be an equalizer in school and the workplace. Technology should be integrated throughout each curriculum area. Moreover, our children must become computer literate and learn how to access information as soon as possible. The difficulty for any teacher or parent will be helping students figure out which information is essential and which is unimportant.

A word about subject areas and passions is in order. One of the authors had an opportunity to attend a Christmas exhibition of arts and crafts to sell or show. While "shopping" through the different booths, the author noticed a small but interested crowd at a booth in which a gentleman was displaying two model airplanes that he had built, each about 4 feet long. The planes were not for sale. They were constructed exquisitely, and the builder (whose vocation had nothing to do with planes) explained with obvious passion how much he enjoyed the hobby and flying the planes. Several times he indicated, with a smile, that the model airplanes were a "disease" and that he just loved the challenge of experimenting and building. We hope that our children develop a passion, a "disease," for a discipline or an integrated conceptualization of several disciplines.

4. What would you hope to see when walking in the school?

When walking in the school, we would anticipate seeing student work displayed frequently and all over the halls. Bulletin boards with examples of what is taking place in classes and schoolwide projects emphasizing academics, art, drama, music, and science ecology projects would tell us that the school is an exciting place in which to learn. The school should be clean, with no graffiti or student locker damage. We would expect to see teachers and students talking together about schoolwork and teachers and students interacting comfortably. Noticing that teachers and administrators know the names of most students would reassure us that a smaller school, or a larger school divided into "houses" or "families," is in the best interest of our children. It would be nice for a teacher, principal, or secretary to say "Hi" with a smile when he or she sees us, asking whether he or she could be of any help.

When passing the cafeteria, we would hope to see students enjoying their lunches and observing students of different ethnic groups together and enjoying one another's company. Seeing a few teachers or administrators interacting positively with the students would be impressive. Although we would expect to sign in at the main office, we would hope that an overly vigilant climate is unnecessary. We would trust that students feel safe in the school. While in the main office, we would expect students to be assisting staff as a school service. Also, teachers and classified staff would be addressing students warmly and appreciatively during office interactions. Hearing the principal call a few students by their first names, and for positive reasons, would be welcome.

A Vision of Professional Development[2]

An essential part of a principal's vision should be dedicated to helping faculty members continue to grow as professionals and involving the teachers in the decisions about their growth. How many principals have ever asked their faculty, "If you could select a specific staff development project to improve your teaching, what would you choose?" Unfortunately, most staff development efforts do not ask this question because the efforts move forward on the premise that all teachers have the same needs and experiences. Effective staff development practices consider the needs and specific job-related responsibilities of each individual. Some school districts are adopting a differentiated approach to supervisory practices in which each staff member is able to identify and pursue professional growth goals in keeping with his or her specific role in the school. Every goal must, in some way, build a capacity to serve students.

Large-Scale Staff Development

If an entire faculty staff development project is considered, then there should be extensive faculty involvement in the selection of options. For example, one school, when bringing a consultant to share ideas on the NCTM standards, corresponded back and forth with the consultant for several months to plan every aspect of the visit including instructional strategies, curriculum information for specific grade levels, particular textbook suggestions, and assessment practices. Faculty ownership of the process created the foundation for a successful visit. The consultant did his homework, which earned him the admiration of the staff.

For a staff development effort to succeed, it is critical to provide sufficient faculty training so that the innovation is not dependent on frequent return visits by the consultant. The training should involve enough staff members so that if a couple of teachers leave, the program does not leave with them. The school administration also should play more than a perfunctory role in the effort. There should be an expectation that the administration, especially those responsible for the grade levels or departments involved, will participate in the training.

Curriculum Review Cycles

A first-rate staff development opportunity exists every time a school or district implements its curriculum review cycle to examine a subject area or adopt new textbooks and instructional resources. Principals need to ensure that interested staff members have the opportunity to work on the project in the district office or at the school site. Again, by having faculty members actively involved in the decision-making process, one is more likely to accept the decisions and gain greater understanding of the concepts and teaching strategies. These teachers will become on-site "experts" on the subject areas reviewed. This level of involvement in the review can only benefit the students and the teacher. Key aspects of the review will include the following:

1. an examination of the school philosophy and mission as it relates to the subject;
2. analysis of the "historical record" on the subject with regard to previous district implementation efforts;
3. review of literature on the subject (e.g., NCTM, National Council of Social Studies, National Council of Teachers of English) and curriculum (e.g., Association for Supervision and Curriculum Development) associations;
4. development of a belief statement on the subject, tailored to district and school needs, to guide selection of resources;
5. ordering of sample textbooks, trade books, and other instructional resources and/or the development of district/school resources;
6. if possible, piloting of the resources in several classes;
7. final selection and adoption of resources for the district and school;
8. instructional and resource inservice of staff on the adopted material;
9. implementation of the new program in the district and school; and
10. yearly monitoring, assessment, and fine-tuning of the program.

Staff Development and Evaluation

Most principals and teachers would not view staff development and evaluation as "partners." The evaluation process is perceived by most teachers as intimidating and of little assistance to their professional growth. Yet, when principals build trust and rapport with faculty and use supervisory practices (e.g., clinical supervision, peer coaching, cognitive coaching) in a nonthreatening way, the practices can become a form of staff development. For example, the experienced teacher can use a pre-observation conference to share reflections about lesson possibilities, fine-tune a lesson, and return after the lesson to use the principal as a springboard for dialogue and perspective sharing.

Differentiated staff development options can take the supervision to the next level by providing experienced staff members with a variety of options to foster their professional growth. To illustrate, differentiated professional growth can include participation in a curriculum review cycle as discussed previously, serving as a mentor teacher to new staff members, reporting to faculty on a summer workshop or conference, participating in action research, sponsoring a faculty reading group (e.g., coping with gangs, charter schools), experimenting with team teaching, participating in a "brown bag" group on technology, participating in a study group, being involved on a site team, coordinating assemblies, organizing faculty meetings, developing strategies for at-risk youngsters, developing strategies for Individuals with Disabilities Education Act or Section 504 students, implementing portfolios, writing an educational grant, and using brain-based research. It is essential that a differentiated professional growth option come from the faculty member and be based on a professional goal. Administration provides support for the effort.

Informal Staff Development

Every day in a school, a principal can promote informal staff development. When a principal asks a teacher how a child is doing, what strategies have been tried, or what has succeeded, the principal is informally "challenging" the teacher to reflect on his or her performance. Sharing an article with faculty about an interesting topic (e.g., pros and cons of distance learning) and encouraging faculty to share articles in return contributes to professional growth. Encouraging teachers to display student work, projects, and investigations outside of their classrooms opens the possibilities for other teachers examining the work and thinking, "How would a similar idea work for my class?" Creating a staff development library, supporting teachers who videotape lessons, supporting brown bag discussions, downlinking satellite broadcasts for the school, and providing a list of Internet educational sites on particular topics all are informal and nonthreatening activities that contribute to a climate of staff development through community, collaboration, and professionalism.

Notes

1. For conventional purposes, we are referring to one elementary school teacher. However, the spirit of the activity applies equally to

the *seven* teachers our children would have, including specialists, in an elementary, middle, or high school.

2. Comprehensive reviews of staff development, supervision, evaluation, and differentiated professional growth options are included in *The Principal's Companion* (Robbins & Alvy, 1995).

CHAPTER 14

The Obvious Is Not Always Obvious: What School Principals Often Forget

Regardless of how much training one receives for a job, one tends to dive in, try his or her best, and, quite often, miss the forest while gazing at the trees; although all principals have the best of intentions, this section covers ideas and strategies that can be easily missed. Some of these ideas might seem obvious to the reader, but based on the personal experiences of school principals, *the obvious is not always obvious*. Hopefully, by sharing these ideas, principals will remember to keep focused on the forest as well as on the trees; in other words, being able to focus on the big picture yet attend to important details is both a challenge and a valuable skill.

Schools Also Are for Adults

> The most important thing is to always be aware of what it's like to have been a teacher. Many principals lose sight of what the classroom is like and the pressures of the classroom.
>
> *A principal's voice*

A principal is so involved in the school mission and in considering the school as a place for children or young adults that it is easy to forget that a school also is a place for adults, both teachers and classified staff members. (Schools also are for parents, and we discuss this later in the chapter.) Initially, it might sound sacrilegious to state that adults in a school are as important as the students. However, if there is a constant emphasis on helping adults in the school reach their potentials and on keeping them professionally fresh and motivated, then students benefit. Typically, a principal is not "trained" to think in this manner. If adults experience a mentally stimulating workplace, then they are more likely to create this same environment in the classroom for students. If adults are not excited about their professional role as teachers, then students are going to notice; teacher enthusiasm is vital for student success. From the beginning, a principal should do what he or she can to generate excitement about teaching, the importance of the profession, and the professional development of the faculty.

If teacher growth is a top priority, then we should recognize that it is just as important to provide teacher in-service on a new reading program as it is to order that program for the children. In practice, priority spending frequently goes for the reading program without regard, or with little regard, to the professional growth needs of teachers. Yet, how often do teachers—even experienced ones—struggle with programs because they were not provided with strategies or resources to make changes. A veteran principal still recalls parents flocking to his office one "open school night" because a teacher indicated to the parents that a new reading program was just too complicated for her.

Displaying Respect Through Faculty Meetings

An effective way in which to recognize that schools are for adults as well as students is by displaying respect for teachers by thoughtfully organizing faculty meetings. A faculty meeting that dwells on "administrivia" that can easily be covered in a memo is disrespectful of faculty members and their time. Each faculty meeting should be a professional growth opportunity and a chance to dignify faculty members by citing specific school and teacher accomplishments and celebrating work well done. The specificity of the principal's remarks will indicate that he or she has noticed the successes and probably will increase the likelihood that these deeds will be repeated.

Teachers and administrators should walk out of a faculty meeting feeling that it was worthwhile and productive. The experience should be similar to how students feel when they walk out of a successful class. This is an indicator of an ethically aligned organization. Adults in a school should be nurtured, just as students should be nurtured. Dignifying the faculty also can be accomplished by having several teachers plan the faculty meeting with the principal. Providing refreshments for staff after a busy day in their classrooms can be a nice touch, as would a few humorous (if appropriate) comments. Also, it is essential for the staff to feel that the principal is at the meeting in body and mind. A principal who, through verbal or nonverbal signals, gives the impression that he or she has more important things to do (e.g., constantly looking at watch or clock) is displaying disrespect and a lack of professional courtesy for the group.

Taking Care of Oneself and the Faculty

It is very difficult to help others if the principal is physically or mentally at risk. It is important to schedule one's time to allow for exercise, family time, and time away from the office. One might think that a good way in which to build credibility with faculty members is for them to see the principal as the "tireless workaholic." In the long run, faculty members would be much better off seeing the principal create balance in his or her life. The Greek notion of moderation might be the best model to avoid personal burnout. Remember, exercise or other personal activities must be scheduled on one's calendar; otherwise, other events will occupy the time. The secretary should know the principal's priorities and the value of maintaining a balanced schedule. Of course, this also means supporting the secretary's desire to leave work at the appropriate time for family and exercise. Ethical alignment runs through the organization.

If you are a parent, it is important for your own peace of mind, as well as the piece of mind of your family, to play a crucial role in the raising of your child. It might seem obvious, but the principal who is a workaholic can easily miss the events and important milestones of his or her own child's life. Ethical alignment means leaving the school at 10 a.m. to travel across town to see your little girl or boy in a school play. Moreover, it means supporting teachers and encouraging them to take personal time to see their children accept awards. Your behavior in these situations can have a strong and positive effect on the school culture. The message is clear: This school is a caring place; we care for our students, our staff families, and each other.

A principal's voice:

Sometimes we spend so much time raising other people's kids that we don't raise our own.

A principal's personal example as a lifelong learner can have a strong influence on faculty and students. For example, a valuable idea can be a principal's suggestion to create a book club giving teachers and classified staff a chance to engage in a voluntary and "laid back" intellectual discussion. The book club could "ignite the burners" of teachers going through difficult periods. Also, teachers should know that the principal hopes they will work hard and play hard. Encouraging staff to exercise, possibly by sponsoring an aerobics group at school (before school, during lunch, or after school), can send a powerful message that the principal cares about the physical and mental well-being of the staff.

A veteran principal recalled the fond memories he has of a superintendent taking several principals out to eat on a Friday afternoon every other month. The setting was nonthreatening, and both school and nonschool topics were up for discussion. This simple and informal activity built administrative morale and let the principals know that the superintendent appreciated their efforts and cared for the administrators in a personal and professional way.

Providing Moral Support

When a school, school family, or community goes through a crisis, there needs to be a representative from the school to express support. A principal is one of the most visible individuals in a school and a critical member of a community. A principal should realize that he or she needs to be there for certain events, even though these events might be sad and tragic. Each of us was raised from childhood with the image of a school principal in our lives. A principal can provide compassion, encouragement, and comfort to others. When a tragedy does occur in a family served by the school, the principal's presence will be perceived as lending the school's support for the family's ordeal. The principal's actions will demonstrate the impact of the tragedy on the whole community.

Fighting the Jump-to-Change Reflex

A principal new to a site might see that significant change is needed. However, it is important to display respect for what a school has accomplished. One needs to know why things are the way they are and analyze the strengths and weaknesses of the system. By reflecting on how things have operated, a leader will be displaying prudence and taking a first step in building support. Taking time to take stock in the end is a valuable tool for change.

Even veteran principals can fall into a trap by failing to identify key cultural norms and trying to implement ideas that might have seemed minor in their previous schools. One veteran principal, after running into constant difficulties with faculty members, in her old school, over seemingly minor changes, developed a simple technique that helped build credibility. The principal, when considering a new idea, asked a few veteran staff members, "Tell me, is this a big deal?" If the staff members said that the change was indeed a big deal, then the principal would do her homework to find out why a seemingly minor change should be a big deal with that faculty. For example, in her previous school, the principal would informally ask teachers during the day to meet with her briefly after school to check up on specific items. The principal noticed, after a few meetings in the new school, that staff members usually were a little nervous when entering her office after school. So, she tested the technique and asked, "Tell me, is this a big deal, meeting after school?" The teachers said, "Yes." Why? Because whenever the previous principal had said she wanted to have a short and informal after-school meeting, it meant that bad news was going to be delivered.

There are times when changes will have to be made immediately. For example, when racist language or assaults are taking place in a school, a principal needs to take an immediate stand for what is right. Sometimes a new principal's personal history, intuition, or emerging vision simply tells him or her that something is terribly wrong and that an immediate change needs to occur. Hopefully, when this is the case, there are members of the faculty and community who have been waiting for the right leader to emerge and take a stand. Even in these cases, it is important to try to rally support. When a principal is new to a school, almost everyone else in the organization understands the culture better than does the principal. Regardless of how right the newcomer might be on an issue, support will be needed from organizational members. Welcome it.

A Vision for Monday Morning

While principals, superintendents, school board members, and consultants are talking about visions and mission statements, teachers are thinking about what they have to teach on Monday morning. Principals need to remember that when asking teachers to work on vision projects, teachers will (and should) ask, "How will this affect our classrooms? Can we spend our time in a more constructive way than sitting in on this vision meeting?" Recognizing the practical concerns of teachers means that the stakes are high when a principal requests their presence at a meeting. Teachers should not be asked to attend a meeting unless the meeting is really meaningful. Teachers should play an active role in any vision-building activity, and language should be included in the vision that really affects what they do in their classrooms. The language should be important enough for all of a school's faculty members to try to implement the objectives in their classrooms. Also, consider timing of such a meeting. There are critical times of the year when teachers need to be able to focus exclusively on their classrooms.

A vision for Monday morning also is a reminder that principals should avoid becoming so absorbed in their schools' futures that they forget about teachers' Monday morning needs. Yes, working on the future is critical, necessary, exciting, intellectually stimulating, and often fun. But principals can show teachers that they care about Monday by making sure that instructional supplies for classes will not become a back-burner concern when they are working on vital mission language for student success. It is easy for principals to lose sight of their "mundane" management responsibilities when working on language that gives them a chance to exercise leadership. Leadership and management go hand in hand.

The Moral Responsibilities of a School Principal to Faculty, Parents, and Students

> There is evidence that a principal's success is linked to his or her ability and motivation to use personal and positional power ethically.
>
> *Curcio and Greene (1992, p. 153)*

What Is Moral Leadership?

Moral leadership is based on an understanding of the principles of right and wrong. Through this understanding, the honorable and conscientious individual chooses a path of behavior. For a moral leader, following this path means not only conducting oneself morally but also recognizing and expecting moral conduct from others. Our best modern example of this leadership behavior might be Gandhi, who inspired a nation to follow a path of nonviolent resistance to free India of British rule. Gandhi and his followers responded nonviolently regardless of provocations by the colonial rulers. Many words embrace the spirit of moral behavior—worthy, ethical, exemplary, fair, just, accountable, integrity, and decency. These words have strong implications for school principals. Principals should be worthy of the responsibility and behave in an ethical and exemplary manner with students, teachers, parents, and community members. Principals must be fair and just in their decisions and stand accountable for their actions. They must display integrity and decency by insisting that all students have opportunities to reach their dreams. In short, moral principals do the right thing.

That is easier said than done. For a principal, it is fair to ask, "What is the right thing?" As a newcomer to a school is learning the ropes and trying to keep the school afloat on a day-to-day basis, it is easy to forget about other things. At times, a principal feels unprepared and loses a bit of self-confidence, direction, and possibly self-esteem. Thus, it is important to write and revisit a purposeful and personal mission statement to remind oneself why he or she became a principal. In *The Power of Ethical Management*, Blanchard and Peale (1988) maintain that for individuals to act ethically, they must be grounded, secure, and confident. "Both of us agree that ethical behavior is related to self-esteem. We both believe that people who feel good about themselves have what it takes to withstand outside pressure and to do what is right rather than do what is merely expedient, popular, or lucrative" (p. 7). Blanchard and Peale's point is critical; to do what is right, it certainly is helpful to feel good about oneself, to have confidence and a direction, and to have purposeful vision to guide one's behavior. The moral responsibility to faculty, parents, and students should be the essence of a principal's leadership vision.

The Moral Responsibility to Faculty

During the past 20 years, historians, political scientists, and organizational behavior theorists have acknowledged with appreciation and gratitude the work of James MacGregor Burns. Burns's (1978) work on transformational leadership is a fascinating, creative, and inspirational document because it describes what we, as leaders and followers, can become. Burns states, "Transforming leadership ultimately becomes *moral* in that it raises the level of human conduct and ethical aspiration of both leader and led, and thus it has a transforming effect on both" (p. 20, emphasis in original). Principals serve students and teachers. In their service to teachers, principals can be transformational leaders by doing everything in their power to help teachers be the best they can be.

A principal might not think of his or her efforts as transformational. But when considering service to teachers and the possibilities of raising "the level of human conduct," one can see the potential influence of the principalship. As one of the most visible individuals in a school, almost every action a principal takes can have moral implications. A comment to a child, a greeting to a parent, a remark to a cafeteria worker, and a walk through the school with the custodian all have symbolic and moral implications because the actions tell us something about the quality of relationships. In the case of faculty members, the quality of the relationship between teachers and the principal will likely have implications for the classrooms. The principal sends a strong message about the quality of relationships when he or she empowers teachers with curriculum decisions during meetings, follows a teacher's advice on how to work with a child, or reflects in a productive dialogue with a teacher during a pre- or post-observation conference.

A positive moral tone for the school should be felt as much by teachers as by students. The moral tone should help create a climate in which teachers are affirmed for engaging in risk-taking behavior to improve their teaching. The trust and rapport that is necessary for staff development, supervision, and differentiated professional growth cannot occur without the teachers thinking, "The principal really wants us to experiment with a new strategy, and it will be okay if it doesn't succeed." A moral climate will view "mistakes" as opportunities for growth. It is a teacher's *right* to grow, and mistakes are part of any growth process. Through constructive and honest feedback, one finds out how he or she is doing and whether the teacher is progressing in his or her craft knowledge and practice. Moreover, "Feedback on results is the number one motivator of people" (Blanchard & Peale, 1988, p. 98).

Appreciation for teacher efforts and the "3,000 decisions they are making each day" should be acknowledged by principals whenever they have an opportunity to honor teachers during major public gatherings. Principals should talk about teacher dedication during Parent-Teacher Association (PTA) meetings, open school nights, graduation, or other public forums. Principals always should show respect for teachers in front of parents and students. It is disheartening to hear stories about principals acting disrespectfully with teachers. In almost all cases, any displeasure could be shared in a respectful and private manner.

Finally, principals should remember that it is a service to empower teachers through democratic leadership. Teacher empowerment does not diminish the role of principals. By exercising shared decision making, collaboration, and building community, principals are improving the quality of their work by shifting to a more collaborative model and moving away from a model that is exemplified in the "loneliness of the principalship." A democratic model that thrives on professional dialogue and the curriculum and instructional expertise of the faculty can only enhance the student experience as knowledge and practice of teaching and learning are increased.

The Moral Responsibility to Parents

Concerning parents, the moral responsibility begins with treating parents as a principal hopes to be treated when the principal visits and interacts with the administration of his or her own child's school. It is simply the Golden Rule. One veteran principal often tells parents, during a meeting about their child in his office, "Each child in the school is our most important student, and that is how we will treat this conference about your child."

Based on this approach, it is critical that principals are honest with parents regarding individual and aggregate student test results and other information related to school performance. Although the information might not be pleasant, parents have a right to know. For example, when sharing information concerning standardized tests, classroom progress, behavioral information, or other performance indicators, it is dishonest and misleading to present only the "good news" (or only the "bad news") to make a point or to avoid a confrontation. This leads to uncomfortable parent meetings in which parents ask, "Why wasn't I informed about these grades [or this incident] earlier?"

In addition, if principals are reporting data to parents in newsletters or during gatherings such as open houses, booster clubs, or PTA meetings, then it is important to give an honest picture of how the school is progressing. Again, this will help to reduce surprises later. Keep in mind that honest reporting also includes the good news. A school should be a community that celebrates when student scores improve, when student experiments and performances are successful, when teams win games, and when students overcome adversity. Newsletters, newspaper articles, television and radio spots, and public appearances all should be used to communicate the school's message.

Middle and high school principals should be very cautious concerning what they say about drug use or violence involving their students. Again, honesty is the only acceptable approach. Although principals would like to tell the public that their schools are "drug free," especially if they have not had any suspensions or expulsions due to drugs for several months, principals should be realistic. If it is more accurate to say that students "no longer have to go through a gauntlet of drug users" to enter the school, then principals should say just that; it might be a major accomplishment. However, principals always must stress that the schools are drug-free zones and that any distribution or use of drugs will not be tolerated.

Parents have a right to spend time in schools. It is a principal's moral responsibility to help parents feel comfortable in the schoolhouse. Sensitivity to parents is important. "For some parents, school was a very unpleasant experience, and the school principal may remind them of memories better forgotten" (Robbins & Alvy, 1995, p. 208). To create a welcoming climate, a principal should avoid using educational jargon with parents (and ask teachers to do the same) and provide parents with the "tools" to play an active role in schools. For example, if the school facilities are available, a "Parent Center" (e.g., conference/family room) for PTA or volunteer work certainly sends a warm signal to parents. The center might include parenting books, videos, or educational resources and supplies to conduct meetings. Parents could use the room when waiting for a conference, to make resources for a class activity, or to review a student's work when volunteering.

The Parent Center could be used for workshops on site-based management or to provide information on curriculum initiatives being piloted in the school. The Parent Center could present faculty with a wonderful setting in which to show parents how to use the new mathematics manipulates or the hands-on science material. A technology teacher could bring a computer into the room to share some multimedia ideas or invite parents into the laboratories. These ideas, by eliminating the mystery surrounding some of the new school curriculum, also will be helpful to parents as they assist their own children with homework. Additional "tools" for parents facilitated by the principal or teachers might include ideas such as suggested questioning strategies to ask during parent conferences, evaluating their children's standardized test scores, understanding the language arts portfolios, or developing a folder of ideas for summer educational activities.

Finally, former mayor of New York, Ed Koch, used to travel around the city asking, "How am I doing?" Principals have a moral obligation to aggressively seek feedback from parents on how the school is doing. Feedback can be gained in multiple ways including needs assessment instruments, parent meetings, meetings with individual families, meetings out in the community, phone conversations, e-mail messages, and faxes. Although polls conducted in the United States reveal that citizens, in general, lack confidence in the nation's public schools, they usually indicate support for, and satisfaction with, their neighborhood schools. Principals need to know whether that support extends to their schools. Most important, it is hoped that the data will provide their schools with helpful information and useful suggestions to improve school programs for students.

The Moral Responsibility to Students

Principals and teachers have the opportunity to serve students. There is no greater compliment than to be remembered years later as the teacher or principal who made a difference in a student's life or to be the principal who helped a struggling first-year teacher to a successful career. Educators are unique as leaders because they perform in a learning community. William J. Bennett, the former Secretary of Education, maintains that teachers and principals, because of their sensitive position with children, must not only teach right and wrong but also serve as examples of right behavior for their students (Bennett, 1988). Bennett quotes theologian Martin Buber to stress this vital point: "The educator is distinct from [all other influences] by his will to take part in the stamping of character and by his consciousness that he represents in the eyes of the growing person a certain selection of what is, a selection of what is 'right,' of what should be" (p. 30). This "stamping of character" is an overwhelming moral responsibility for educators.

It is the moral responsibility of all principals to do their part in helping each child in their schools reach his or her potential. Principals need to constantly fight for equal access to the best facilities and the best instructional and human resources for *all* students. Although hiring practices vary greatly from district to district, principals should try to play an active role in the hiring decisions to bring the best teachers to their schools. Again, a bottom-line question should be, "Do I want that teacher for my child?"

When issues of tenure arise, the question should be, "Can we do better for our students?" If a veteran teacher is not doing the job, then a principal should do his or her best to facilitate the teacher through an assistance plan. If that does not work, then the veteran should be counseled out of the profession or, as a last resort, district procedures for contract nonrenewal should be implemented. Contract nonrenewal often is the most difficult and time-consuming aspect of a principal's job. But, if a teacher is damaging students, then contract non-renewal is the ethical thing to do.

Setting a moral tone in a school means that a principal will, by example, show respect for students and help to create a caring and democratic community in and out of the classroom. Although age and maturity play an important role in the range of democratic opportunities open to students, a principal should encourage teachers to begin some democratic activities as early as kindergarten. Democratic activities are not limited to a civics lesson and the social studies curriculum. They can be realized as part of any subject in which students have opportunities to solve problems and make decisions about their own learning. In class, students should have the opportunity to take risks in their learning and express ideas individually and collaboratively. In ethically aligning the school beyond the classroom, a principal and teachers should encourage students to play a role in schoolwide decisions, especially through an active student government.

Building a strong academic program also is critical for a moral leader. The principal always must ask, "How will this program benefit our students?" and "What do our students need to learn?" (as opposed to "What is it that teachers would like to teach?"). Expectations for all students should be high, and the curriculum should not be "watered down" for minority children. The principal must be perceived as fair in his or her behavior with all students regardless of gender, race, religion, or ethnic origin. The principal must ensure that gender or race does not limit a student's opportunity in a course or affect how teachers respond to students. All children must know that they have equal access to the administration and that the principal will be their advocate, although at times that advocacy might be difficult to perceive.

In creating a moral community, a principal must remember that academic success does not ensure that people will care for one another today or in the future. The authors distinctly remember hearing Harvard University psychologist Robert Coles address this issue in a keynote speech during an Association for Supervision and Curriculum Development annual conference. Coles asked his audience to consider the following question: Which nation had the highest literacy rate in 1933? The answer was Nazi Germany. There are no guarantees that literacy will produce caring, kind, and loving persons. Literacy by itself does not ensure moral behavior.

Bill Goetter, education department chair at Eastern Washington University, emphasized that we cannot forget the hope that schooling in a democratic setting holds for each precious individual. As we talk about creating and building community, we should not lose sight of the global dream to emancipate each individual to have the opportunity to be free of physical, intellectual, and spiritual bondage. As the Soviet Union slowly crumbled, millions were freed of the physical and spiritual Gulag. They can now speak their mind, free to express ideas in a new experiment—an open Russian society.

When a woman or child from a village in India fights the bondage of caste or a forced marriage to attend school and learn to read and write, she becomes a bright light for individual freedom. In our American schools, in a society that takes democracy and freedom for granted, we must remember that freedom is a priceless gift and that the 200-year American experience still is an experiment. Experiments do not always succeed. Together in schools and communities, teachers, principals, and parents must nurture the tender soul of each child. Our students, individually and together, must be given the opportunities of freedom—to smile, to play, and to develop their minds—as we continue the emancipation of each child in our global family.

References

Adami, R., & Norton, M. (1996, April). Not in my school you don't! Preventing violence in the middle level school. *NASSP Bulletin,* pp. 19-23. (National Association of Secondary School Principals)

Ahlgren, A., & Kesidou, S. (1995). Attempting curriculum coherence in Project 2061. In *Toward a coherent curriculum: The 1995 ASCD yearbook.* Alexandria, VA: Association for Supervision and Curriculum Development.

Alvy, H. (1983). *The problems of new principals.* Unpublished doctoral dissertation, University of Montana, Missoula.

Alvy, H. (1997, Spring-Summer). Interns offer insights into principalship. *The Principal News,* pp. 11-13. (Association of Washington School Principals).

Alvy, H., & Coladarci, T. (1985). Problems of the novice principal. *Research in Rural Education, 3*(1), 39-47.

American Association for the Advancement of Science. (1990). *Science for all Americans (Project 2061).* Washington, DC: Author.

Aquila, F., & Petzke, J. (1994). *Education law.* Santa Monica, CA: Casenotes Publishing.

Armistead, L. (1996, April). What to do before the violence happens: Designing the crisis communication plan. *NASSP Bulletin,* pp. 31-37.

Association of Washington School Principals. (1996, June). *The principal in . . . Olympia* (Bulletin No. 6). Olympia, WA: Author.

Bennett, W. J. (1988, December). Moral literacy and the formation of character. *NASSP Bulletin,* pp. 29-34. (National Association of Secondary School Principals)

Bennis, W., & Nanus, B. (1985). *Leaders . . . the strategies for taking charge.* New York: Harper & Row.

Blanchard, K., & Peale, N. V. (1988). *The power of ethical management.* New York: William Morrow.

Blumberg, A., & Greenfield, W. (1980). *The effective principal.* Boston: Allyn & Bacon.

Bridges, E. M. (1976, March). Administrative preparation: A critical appraisal. *Thrust,* pp. 3-8.

Brubaker, D. (1995, November). How the principalship has changed. *NASSP Bulletin,* pp. 88-95. (National Association of Secondary School Principals)

Burke, E., & Herbert, D. (1996, April). Zero tolerance policy: Combating violence in schools. *NASSP Bulletin,* pp. 49-54. (National Association of Secondary School Principals)

Burns, J. M. (1978). *Leadership.* New York: Harper & Row.

Burrup, P. (1977). *Financing education in a climate of change.* Boston: Allyn & Bacon.

Caine, R., & Caine, G. (1991). *Making connections, teaching and the human brain.* Alexandria, VA: Association for Supervision and Curriculum Development.

Canady, R. L., & Rettig, M. D. (1995, November). The power of innovative scheduling. *Educational Leadership, 53*(3), 4-10.

Checkley, K. (1996, August). The new union. *Education Update, 38*(5), 1-8. (Association for Supervision and Curriculum Development)

Coladarci, A. P., & Getzels, J. W. (1955). *The use of theory in educational administration.* Educational Administration Monograph No. 5, Stanford University.

Covey, S. R. (1989). *The seven habits of highly effective people.* New York: Simon & Schuster.

Curcio, J., & Greene, E. (1992). Working through "crises of integrity." In F. Parkay & G. Hall (Eds.), *Becoming a principal* (chap. 7). Boston: Allyn & Bacon.

Daly-Lewis, J. (1987, September). Getting through Year One. *Principal,* pp. 36-38.

Daresh, J. (1993, April). *The arrival of the new principal: Reactions of staff.* Paper presented at the meeting of the American Educational Research Association, Atlanta, GA.

Darling-Hammond, L. (1996). The right to learn and the advancement of teaching: Research, policy, and practice for democratic education. *Educational Researcher, 25*(6), 5-17.

Deal, T. (1985). Cultural change: Opportunity, silent killer, or meta-morphosis? In R. Kilmann, M. Saxton, & R. Serpa (Eds.), *Gaining control of the corporate culture* (chap. 15, pp. 292-331). San Francisco: Jossey-Bass.

Deal, T., & Peterson, K. (1994). *The leadership paradox.* San Francisco: Jossey-Bass.

Donmoyer, R., Imber, M., & Scheurich, J. (1995). *The knowledge base in educational administration.* Albany: State University of New York Press.

Drucker, P. (1992). *Managing for the future.* New York: Truman Talley Books.

Duke, D., Isaacson, N., Sagor, R., & Schmuck, R. (1984). *Transition to leadership.* Portland, OR: Lewis and Clark College, Educational Administration Program.

Foley, J. (1996, September). Starting from scratch in a new school. *Principal,* pp. 50-51.

Frizzel, G. K. (1995, October). *Working with unions.* Paper presented at seminar on educational administration, Eastern Washington University, Cheney.

Fullan, M., & Stiegelbauer, S. (1991). *The new meaning of educational change.* New York: Columbia University, Teachers College Press.

Gamble, C. (1996, August 7). Pennsylvania community mourns after losing 16 students, 5 adults in TWA crash. *Education Week,* p. 10.

Garberina, M. R. (1980, December). *Rites of passage: Role socialization among novice principals.* Paper presented at the Annual Meeting of the American Anthropological Association, Washington, DC.

Gardner, H. (1985). *Frames of mind: The theory of multiple intelligences.* New York: Basic Books.

Gardner, H. (1995). *Leading minds: An anatomy of leadership.* New York: Basic Books.

Goleman, D. (1995). *Emotional intelligence.* New York: Bantam Books.

Gorton, R. A. (1980). *School administration.* Dubuque, IA: William C. Brown.

Gorton, R. A., & Snowden, P. (1993). *School leadership and administration.* Madison, WI: Brown & Benchmark.

Goss v. Lopez, 419 U.S. 565 (1975).

Hall, G., & Mani, M. (1992). Entry strategies: Where do I begin? In F. Parkay & G. Hall (Eds.), *Becoming a principal* (chap. 2). Boston: Allyn & Bacon.

Hart, A. (1993). *Principal succession.* Albany: State University of New York Press.

Hartzell, G., Williams, R., & Nelson, K. (1995). *New voices in the field.* Thousand Oaks, CA: Corwin.

Heller, G. S. (1996, April). Changing the school to reduce student violence: What works? *NASSP Bulletin,* pp. 1-10. (National Association of Secondary School Principals)

Hill, M. (1996, April). Making students part of the safe schools solution. *NASSP Bulletin,* pp. 24-30. (National Association of Secondary School Principals)

Houghton Mifflin. (1976). *The American heritage dictionary of the English language* (new college ed.). Boston: Author.

House, E. (1996). A framework for appraising educational reforms. *Educational Researcher. 25*(7), 7-14.

Hoy, W., & Miskel, C. (1996). *Educational administration theory, research and practice.* New York: McGraw-Hill.

Hughes, L. W., & Ubben, G. C. (1989). *The elementary principal's handbook.* Boston: Allyn & Bacon.

Iller, R. (1996a). *Can you be liable for injuries to a student?* Unpublished manuscript, Whitworth College, Spokane, WA.

Iller, R. (1996b). *School officials, law enforcement agencies and searches of students.* Unpublished manuscript, Whitworth College, Spokane, WA.

Jentz, B. C. (1982). *Entry.* New York: McGraw-Hill.

Johnson, C. K., & Lombard, M. (1996, September 8). Principals too reluctant to criticize. *Spokesman Review,* pp. A1, A10-A11. (Spokane, WA)

Johnson, D. W., & Johnson, R. T. (1996, April). Reducing school violence through conflict resolution training. *NASSP Bulletin,* pp. 11-18. (National Association of Secondary School Principals)

Kaiser, J. (1995). *The 21st century principal.* Mequon, WI: Stylex.

Kohn, A. (1996). *Beyond discipline: From compliance to community.* Alexandria, VA: Association for Supervision and Curriculum Development.

Lawton, M. (1996, October 30). Study: Site management has no effect on scores. *Education Week.* p. 7.

Litke, C. D. (1996). When violence came to our rural school. *Educational Leadership, 54*(1), 77-80.

Louis, M. R. (1980, June). Surprise and sense making: What newcomers experience in entering unfamiliar organizational settings. *Administrative Science Quarterly, 25,* 226-251.

Lyman, L., Eskildsen, L., Frank, J., Nunn, C., O'Day, D., & O'Donnell, S. (1993). Female principals: Change credibility and gender. *Planning and Change, 24*(1,2), 30-40.

Mascaro, F. G. (1973). Early on-the-job socialization of first-year elementary school principals. *Dissertation Abstracts International, 34,* 7492A. (Doctoral dissertation, University of California, Riverside)

McGregor, D. (1960). *The human side of enterprise.* New York: McGraw-Hill.

Miklos, E. (1988). Administrative selection, career patterns, succession and socialization. In N. Boyan (Ed.), *Handbook of research on educational administration* (chap. 3). New York: Longman.

Murphy, J., & Pimentel, S. (1996, September). Grading principals: Administrator evaluations come of age. *Kappan, 78*(1), 74-81.

Naisbitt, J. (1982). *Megatrends.* New York: Warner Books.

New Jersey v. TLO, 469 U.S. 325 (1985).

Nichols, M. (1995). *The lost art of listening.* New York: Guilford.

Olson, L. (1996a, September 4). Leadership standards target teaching, learning. *Education Week,* p. 5.

Olson, L. (1996b, September 11). 25 years brings world of change for veteran Virginia educator. *Education Week,* p. 9.

Osterman, K., Crow, G., & Rosen, J. (1993, April). *New principals: Problems, priorities and preparation.* Paper presented at the meeting of the American Educational Research Association, Atlanta, GA.

Parkay, F., Currie, G., Rhodes, J., & Rao, M. (1992). Beginning principals: Who are they? What are their priorities? In F. Parkay & G. Hall (Eds.), *Becoming a principal* (chap. 1). Boston: Allyn & Bacon.

Parkay, F., & Hall, G. (Eds.). (1992). *Becoming a principal.* Boston: Allyn & Bacon.

Peterson, K. (1982). Making sense of principals' work. *Australian Administrator, 3*(3), 1-4.

Robbins, P., & Alvy, H. (1995). *The principal's companion.* Thousand Oaks, CA: Corwin.

Roberts, J. & Wright, L. (1992). Initiating change. In F. Parkay & G. Hall (Eds.), *Becoming a principal* (chap. 6, pp. 130-136). Boston: Allyn & Bacon.

Ryan, K., & Cooper, J. (1995). *Those who can, teach.* Boston: Houghton Mifflin.

Sarason, S. B. (1982). *The culture of the school and the problem of change.* Boston: Allyn & Bacon.

Schein, E. H. (1974). Organizational socialization and the profession of management. In D. Kolb, I. Rubin, & J. McIntyre (Eds.), *Organizational psychology.* Englewood Cliffs, NJ: Prentice Hall.

Sergiovanni, T. (1992). *Moral leadership.* San Francisco: Jossey-Bass.

Shakeshaft, C. (1995). A cup half full: A gender critique of the knowledge base in educational administration. In R. Donmoyer, M. Imber, & J. Scheurich (Eds.), *The knowledge base in educational administration* (pp. 139-157). Albany: State University of New York Press.

Shelton, M. (1991, March). Mentoring: Lending a hand to tomorrow's principals. *Principal,* p. 16.

Skelly, K. (1996, February). A letter to a newly appointed principal: Ten tips for making the grade. *NASSP Bulletin,* pp. 90-96. (National Association of Secondary School Principals)

Thomson, S. (Ed.). (1993). *Principals for our changing schools: The knowledge and skill base.* Lancaster, PA: Technomic.

Watkins, H., & Olzendam, A. (1996, October). *Rebuilding confidence between a school and a community.* Paper presented at seminar at Whitworth College, Spokane, WA.

Willis, S. (1996, November). Redefining school leadership. *Education Update, 38*(7), 4. (Association For Supervision and Curriculum Development)

Wulff, K., with Williams, R. (1996). *The changing role of the principal* (executive summary). Olympia: Association of Washington School Principals.

Index